DEADLY
MAGIC

DEADLY MAGIC

A Personal Account of Communications
Intelligence in World War II in the Pacific

Edward Van Der Rhoer

CHARLES SCRIBNER'S SONS / NEW YORK

Library of Congress Cataloging in Publication Data

Van Der Rhoer, Edward.
  Deadly magic.

  1. World War, 1939–1945 — Cryptography.   2. World
War, 1939–1945 —Personal narratives, American.   3. Van
Der Rhoer, Edward.   4. United States. Office of Naval
Communications —Biography.   5. Seamen —United States —
Biography.   6. World War, 1939–1945 —United States.
7. World War, 1939–1945 —Pacific Ocean.   I. Title.
D810.C88V36   940.54′86   78-17120
ISBN 0-684-15873-6

No other people, as a whole, is entirely our enemy.
No people at all— not even ourselves— is entirely
our friend.

GEORGE F. KENNAN

Contents

Prologue   *1*

1. Marching to a Distant Drum   *10*

2. When the Harvard Yard Went to War   *24*

3. Climb the Highest Mountain   *46*

4. Visions Before Midnight   *70*

5. Blood-Red Sun over a Picture-Book Island   *104*

6. Those Who Dwell in the Dust   *134*

7. The War of the Marus   *152*

8. Island Hopping: Grim Military Hopscotch   *164*

9. The Last Throw of the Dice   *178*

10. Downfall   *194*

11. The End of a Time of Troubles   *205*

INDEX   *217*

List of Illustrations

Boylston Hall, Harvard University   25

Edward Van Der Rhoer, 1941   30

Dave Huggins, Jack Hall, and "McKinnon-san"   39

The author and James Philip Kearny   47

Commander Redfield Mason   51

The Navy Department Building, Washington, D.C.   68

Fleet Admiral Isoroku Yamamoto   89

Admiral Chuichi Nagumo   91

A page from a Japanese code book   95

Japanese carrier *Akagi*   97

Japanese carrier *Hiryu*   100

Admiral Raizo Tanaka   117

Japanese prisoner, Guadalcanal   131

LIST OF ILLUSTRATIONS

Charlotte Whelan Van Der Rhoer   *150*

Sinking of the *Nittsu Maru*   *157*

Sinking of the *Teiko Maru*   *159*

Marines at Tarawa   *168*

The *Yamato* under attack   *200*

Explosion aboard the *Yamato*   *201*

DEADLY
MAGIC

Prologue

Seldom has a nation become involved in war with less forethought and more complacency than the United States entered the Second World War. Franklin D. Roosevelt was preparing the country for war with Nazi Germany, but even the president did not expect to enter that war through the back door—by provoking Japan into direct aggression against the United States. One wonders what might have happened if Hitler had not obliged his Far Eastern ally (and Roosevelt!) by promptly declaring war on the United States. After all, Japan never succumbed to Hitler's blandishments to join the Germans in *their* war against the Soviet Union.

Hypnotized by the war in Europe, which was viewed, correctly enough, as the most dangerous threat to American security, Washington directed its Pacific diplomacy with all the insouciance of a symphony conductor whose attention is riveted on the strings and who ignores the sour notes in the brass section. Thus the top leadership in Washington followed developments in the Far East with only half an eye and, even when forewarned about the critical stage of those developments, wrongheadedly concluded that Japan's aggressive moves were aimed southward into the area of Indochina and the Dutch East Indies or against the Soviet Union in the Siberian Maritime Provinces and hence posed no immediate threat to the United States. No one from Roosevelt on down through the cabinet and the upper echelons of government seriously dwelled on the possibility that the most stunning blow of the Japanese aggression might be delivered at the stronghold of the U.S. Pacific Fleet in Pearl Harbor. Gen. Walter C. Short and Adm. H. E. Kimmel in Hawaii shared in this general lack of foresight (although it was more understandable in their cases since they had only part of the picture) but became the principal scapegoats, if only because, in wartime, a nation cannot afford to indict its entire leadership. Scapegoats had to be found in order to placate an American people deeply shocked by the way in which its defenses had been so easily caught off guard.

It has been said that military leaders always prepare for the next war on the basis of their experience in the last one, thereby suggesting that the inclination of generals and admirals is to look backward rather than forward. (Perhaps a similar inclination led the French General Staff to build the Maginot Line after their experience with static trench warfare in World War I.) While there may be an element of truth in such a statement, it has also been said with some truth that those who fail to learn from the past are destined to relive it. Indeed our leaders seemed to have taken little account of Japanese behavior in earlier national crises, and for their sin of omission our nation paid a heavy price. But in the context of the present moment in history, it is more to the point to wonder whether we do not tend to prepare for the enemy action with which we have grown more familiar, at least in our thoughts and assessments, and hence to ignore what is unfamiliar or strange to us on the mistaken ground that this is in consequence less likely to happen.

The Japanese government planned to have its two envoys in

Washington deliver the note breaking off negotiations with the United States on December 7, 1941, at 1:00 P.M. Washington time, which was dawn in Hawaii, when torpedo planes and dive bombers from the Japanese carrier task force would be launching their strikes at Pearl Harbor. Because of a delay in deciphering and retyping the final, fourteenth part of the message, Ambassadors Saburo Kurusu and Kichisaburo Nomura were an hour late in delivering this note, and by the time they arrived, Secretary of State Cordell Hull had already been advised by the president of the Pearl Harbor attack. Thus the Japanese did not formally break off negotiations until after the attack on Pearl Harbor. Still it remained typical of the Japanese not to worry too much about diplomatic formalities like a declaration of war, and no one on our side should have been really surprised one way or the other.

Adm. Isoroku Yamamoto, who masterminded the Imperial Navy's sneak attack on the principal U.S. naval base in the Pacific, was a great admirer of his predecessor, Adm. Heihachiro Togo, naval hero of the Russo-Japanese War. Negotiations had dragged on between Russia and Japan for half a year before they were broken off on February 5, 1904. On the fourth the Japanese had already decided to resort to force, and as usual they coordinated their diplomacy with their military preparations, seeing to it that the former lagged slightly behind the latter. Although war was not declared until the tenth, on February 8 the main battle fleet commanded by Admiral Togo struck at Port Arthur, one of the principal stations of the Russian fleet. The Russian Far Eastern Fleet never recovered from this blow, and Russia's defeat at sea was finally sealed when Togo surprised the Baltic Fleet as it passed through the Tsushima Strait, hoping to reinforce the Far Eastern Fleet, and brought about its nearly complete destruction.

In this war Japan had realistically waged a limited type of hostilities against Russia, never misleading itself with the dream of defeating Russia at home, thousands of miles away, but aiming only at establishing its supremacy in the Far East and forcing Russia to sue for peace. In this aim Japan was aided, ironically, by the

United States when President Theodore Roosevelt decided to push Russia into peace negotiations that were settled largely on Japan's terms.

On the eve of our involvement in World War II, the United States enjoyed the tremendous advantage of its "Magic"—the reading of Japanese diplomatic codes or, more particularly, the machine cipher known as PURPLE—and yet, as it turned out, derived little or no benefit from this advantage during the protracted negotiations leading up to the outbreak of war. Through its obtuseness, Washington saw only what it wanted to see or whatever happened to fit in with the preconceived and mutually reinforced ideas of the top governmental bureaucracy.

Our ability to read Japan's cryptographic communications—military as well as diplomatic—helped us, however, to recover from the savage enemy onslaught much more quickly than we had a right to expect. Although Yamamoto said, according to one version of his remarks, that peace with the United States would require the Japanese forces to march into Washington and sign the peace treaty in the White House, there is no evidence that the Japanese leaders really believed in such an outcome. Their underlying idea seems to have been a result not unlike that of the Russo-Japanese War, though on a much broader scale. It would be forced upon the United States not only by the realistic military and naval position in the Pacific but also by Nazi Germany's domination of the European continent. According to this plan, the outer perimeter of the Japanese-controlled Pacific would be pushed as far south as Australia and as far east as Hawaii. Loss of the Hawaiian Islands would eliminate the U.S. presence in the mid-Pacific and force an American retreat of two thousand miles to the West Coast of the United States. Japan could then consolidate its gains and wait for Washington to recognize the futility of waging a costly and unpromising war in the Pacific, especially in view of the fact that a still more dangerous adversary, Hitler's Germany, was in its rear.

Only the massive, incredibly productive code-breaking efforts of the U.S. Navy's OP-20-G frustrated these Japanese aims in the Pacific. In the early stages of the war when we were still reeling from their blows, we succeeded in concentrating our depleted forces to meet the next attacks at precisely the right time and place—no small advantage in the vast reaches of the Pacific where we could not possibly guard every point.

During all the years of the war I was one of the privileged few who remained at the heart of the American code-breaking enterprise that made it possible to foresee nearly every move of the formidable Japanese enemy. In this way I found myself in a position to see the "grand design" about which the average fighting man could know little or nothing. As James Jones wrote: "There was no way for him to know. Strategic aims and planning, for simple reasons of security, could not be handed down to the rank and file. Even if he knew them, they wouldn't change his life much, or what he had to do. . . ."

As our strength grew, we pursued our "grand design" with the island-hopping campaign that enabled us to penetrate deeper and deeper into the Japanese stronghold. It was to a large extent a naval war, not only because the commitment of sizable ground forces in the Pacific would have been at best a difficult affair, but also because in commitments Roosevelt made to the British even before we became a participant, the number-one priority was given to Europe. Yet we continued to make progress after the first year when we had all we could do to hold our own. At each step of the way we knew, through our breaking of the enemy codes, what the Japanese were trying to do in the way of countermoves. We could determine the results of our attacks, not by our own side's estimates (which always tend to exaggerate their effectiveness) but by the enemy's reports to higher commanders, which generally do not inflate losses. We knew both their strengths and their weaknesses. And during the entire period we watched their resupply activities and kept hammering away at Japan's merchant marine, learning most of their ship movements from their codes and dispatching our submarines to the exact noon positions in order to destroy their convoys. Near the end of the war, the Japanese merchant marine had been practically wiped out and the reinforcement of the empire had become an impossibility. Their tankers were also wiped out and the Japanese fleet finally had to be divided in order to keep the heavy surface units close to oil supplies, thus considerably limiting its remaining effectiveness.

At the very last, PURPLE came into its own again, making us aware that the Japanese, relying on their Treaty of Neutrality with the Soviet Union, were seeking peace through Moscow's mediation. As a result, we remained on guard at the Potsdam Conference with Stalin and Molotov and avoided the trap of offering the USSR further concessions à la Yalta in order to induce it to join the war against Japan. Had we done otherwise, we would probably have had Soviet forces participating in the occupation of Japan, with consequences analogous to the situation in postwar Germany.

It has become the fashion to denigrate intelligence in the light of the abuses—some real, some only the product of overactive imaginations—charged against the Central Intelligence Agency and the FBI in the aftermath of the Watergate scandal. No doubt intelligence agencies are capable of abuses and may be successful in hiding or concealing them because of related secrecy and security. It would be foolish and dangerous not to try to prevent or reduce the occurrences of such abuses. But the achievements that saved us from the disastrous situation we faced after Pearl Harbor were possible only because dedicated and patriotic Americans had worked so hard before the war to give us access to the information that was absolutely essential to our survival. A horrible example of what can happen when we deprive ourselves of such information is provided by Alexander Kerensky, who, in an excess of idealism, abolished all the Russian intelligence services after the overthrow of the czarist regime. He found himself without reliable information of any sort and was thus rendered helpless to prevent the Bolshevik coup d'etat of November 1917. The Bolsheviks wasted no time, of course, in reestablishing intelligence services, employing some of the same personnel, after they seized power.

Other critics have pointed to the so-called Pearl Harbor mentality which stresses preparedness against surprise attack and have objected to some of its paranoid manifestations. Nevertheless, it would be foolish to disparage preparedness in an age when we have perhaps only minutes to get ready for a devastating thermonuclear attack. It is indispensable to try to learn our potential enemies' intentions—and not merely their capabilities—so that we will have maximum warning about a possible attack. Reading their codes is one of the best ways to find out their intentions.

A few students of cryptanalysis believe that the breaking of codes and ciphers as it occurred during World War II is no longer possible in our time. They cite in support of their case the development of far more sophisticated cipher machines that cannot be attacked by the old cryptanalytical methods. They also assert that the wider use of one-time pads in cryptographic communications ensures that such systems cannot be broken and therefore drastically reduces the value of cryptanalysis.

This seems to me an overpessimistic view of the situation. Communications are even more important today than they were yesterday, and as long as communications exist, outsiders will find means of gaining access to them. Cryptanalysts have not stood still either, and apart from their skills, which on the whole are greater than ever before, they can also make use of tools that did not exist in an earlier period. Thus the pessimists overlook the vastly superior high-speed computers that enable today's cryptanalysts to perform operations unknown to their colleagues several decades ago.

Where human ingenuity alone does not suffice, cryptanalysts can be aided by other means. Agents, defectors, and others turning to foreign governments for reasons of their own will continue surreptitiously to provide cryptographic materials such as codes and ciphers and their keys, information on machine systems, or even the machines themselves, as well as the plain texts of secret messages that are bound to be of great value to cryptanalysts. Sometimes these materials have been stolen by outsiders; at other times they have fallen into the hands of unauthorized people by accident.

There is no reason to suppose that those circumstances may not arise again in the future.

The majority of World War II historians conclude that America's overwhelming superiority in productive capacity and manpower would have won the war sooner or later. Be that as it may, it has been conservatively estimated that our code breaking shortened the war in the Pacific by at least a year. The estimate is open to question on other grounds, however, for without code breaking the war might have developed according to the Japanese plan described above, rather than any of our own, and created a situation entirely adverse to our interest.

The story I present here is a personal one that will help to convey to the reader more vividly, perhaps, than impersonal history the essence in human terms of this tremendous enterprise. Since I served in the United States Navy, my viewpoint is necessarily parochial in that it is slanted toward naval communications intelligence; moreover, it involves only that part of naval communications with which I am best acquainted, the part directed against Japan. The very active effort of the same kind directed against Germany does not belong to this story.

In actuality, several thousands of people participated in the U.S. code-breaking activities under both army and navy auspices. It is to be regretted that writers who have addressed themselves to this subject have tended to focus attention on individuals as if their contributions, however great, could be viewed in isolation from the numerous unknown ones that gave shape and substance to the whole accomplishment. What is more, no one unit at any given geographical spot can be viewed apart from other units engaged in the same work: it was a great collective effort.

For several years the U.S. Navy occupied the center of the stage in the Pacific because, as I have said, the war against Japan was primarily a naval war. This does not in any way detract from the achievements in Gen. Douglas MacArthur's theater in Australia—the pincer reaching north toward the Philippines. But it too depended for its island hopping on naval power. Therefore an account such as mine, which concentrates on naval communications intelligence, tells the story of the whole war in the Pacific while it also gives insight into other operations of the war on a worldwide scale.

I must make it clear that in these personal reminiscences I rely almost exclusively on my own memory of the events in which I personally took part. For obvious reasons I kept no diary and possess no documentary files. I have tried wherever possible to confirm the facts in published historical sources; this is simple enough of course when there is no doubt about the events. But I have found that many published sources contain errors about known facts, while some writers treating naval communications intelligence in their works have made statements that are at variance with my own firsthand knowledge or have given certain facts what is in my opinion a mistaken emphasis.

I am naturally very much aware that one's memory is far from infallible, particularly as events recede farther and farther into the past. Nevertheless, where there is a disagreement between another author's research and my recollections, I have tried to resolve this disagreement by reexamining my memory of the event and only held to my own view if I remain convinced that my memory is accurate. I apologize to the reader in advance for any inaccuracies or outright errors that may have resulted from faulty memory.

In any event, the story I have to tell may illuminate not only the past but also the uncertain future that will become our past in due course.

Marching to a Distant Drum

W ASHINGTON shimmered in the grip of summer heat as the old-fashioned streetcar rattled along unfamiliar streets on its way to the center of the city from Union Station. To a New Yorker like myself Washington appeared to be a sleepy little town. I had heard that the old Ford's Theater where Lincoln was assassinated still stood somewhere in the area through which the streetcar made its way, but I failed to catch a glimpse of anything remotely resemblir g pictures of the theater I had seen. Having nothing better to do, I looked at the headlines of the news-papers other passengers were reading with unusual concentration. German troops continued to roll ahead on a broad front as towns with strange Russian names, many of them unpronounceable, not just Minsk and Pinsk, fell like bowling pins before the onrushing tanks of the invaders.

War in that summer of 1941 in the tranquil capital of the nation seemed far off. Although Hitler was acting in character when he launched his treacherous attack, I did not share the popular view that by this act Stalin had somehow been transformed into a great national hero, the savior of his people, and that *all* Russians were brothers under the skin of the beleaguered forces of democracy fighting in the West. I could not forget the purges in which millions had lost their lives or the show trials that plumbed new depths of hypocrisy or, as the ultimate touch of evil, Stalin's pact with Hitler in 1939, which had unleashed the dogs of war against the West.

Sitting in the streetcar with these thoughts going through my head, I remembered how Churchill had reacted to Hitler's impending invasion of the USSR. He promised all possible aid to the Soviet regime, saying: "If Hitler invaded Hell, I would make at least a favorable reference to the Devil in the House of Commons."

Certainly no one could deny that Nazi Germany constituted a far greater threat to the world now. But if we survived this threat, was it possible that Churchill's "pact with the devil" would lead to an even deadlier peril? No wonder that the Soviet leaders doubted the sincerity of Western support from the beginning. For if the positions had been reversed, they would have chosen to let the other adversaries bleed themselves white, just as they had chosen to sign the pact with Hitler in the hope that Germany and the Western Allies would exhaust themselves in an all-out war, leaving the Soviet Union to dictate the final peace in the midst of the ruins and the dead.

Yet when I looked at those headlines and at the indifferent faces behind the newspapers, as if people were reading the latest big-league baseball scores, the whole war seemed very far away and hardly mattered much. I joined them in their indifference and turned my gaze to the pedestrians and the shops we were passing. All of it looked very different from New York City, where I had lived from childhood. The passersby moved more slowly, with vague deliberateness, the men in shirt-sleeves, lean and loose-boned, like country cousins, the women less chic and stylish than the ones I was used to seeing in New York. Most of the younger men and women were bareheaded while the more mature men wore straw hats and their wives broad-brimmed creations in white or pastel shades.

The buildings we passed, most of them low, seldom higher than three or four stories, reminded me more of Jamaica, Long Island, than the big city. We came to some taller buildings, perhaps ten stories or so, in the middle of town. It hardly appeared to be a very bustling capital for any nation. Then the streetcar rounded a corner, moving at the same leisurely pace, and stopped to discharge passengers on an island in the street. For the first time I saw something distinctive, a marble edifice in the Greek style with tall Corinthian columns which I took to be a government building. Then the streetcar went on, rattling past the front of the White House, which I recognized with a start, for in spite of its familiarity it somehow overwhelmed me when I saw it for the first time in reality. The White House was on my left, separated from me only by an iron fence and an expanse of fine green lawn bordered with flower beds, shaded by noble trees. I hardly noticed Lafayette Park across the avenue.

This sight brought me back to the purpose of my visit to Washington. Just a few days earlier I had received a letter on impressive Navy Department stationery inviting me to come to Washington. While I looked forward to the interview I was about to have, I could not help recalling now the years of preparation that had led up to this moment—one that seemed certain to be a turning point in my life.

Foreign languages had always possessed a special fascination for me. Perhaps this was because I am one of those Americans who are just one generation away from forebears in Europe. All my relatives on my mother's side were German, and they not only made frequent use of their native language in the new country but continued to observe many of the old traditions. My father was Dutch, and his father was a businessman with interests all over Europe. His mother came from a family of intellectuals, *her* father having been a professor, as one would guess at a glance from his photograph. At the same time the city of New York itself, a melting pot, still reflected the pasts of the immigrants whom it had taken in. So I grew up with an acute awareness of the countries beyond the sea which, for me, still held a certain glamor.

In high school on Staten Island I lost myself in a romantic vision of Spain, taking three years of Spanish in preference to other languages like Latin, whose value to anyone interested in Romance languages did not become clear to me until later, and French, which for no discernible reason did not appeal to me at the time. I expected to spend a year in Spain, and only a last-minute change in plans prevented me from being caught there by the civil war.

During my early childhood my mother defied the conventions of her time by obtaining a divorce and remarrying. Her second husband had always sought adventure, the more dangerous the better, and was attracted to the big gamble, whatever it might be. He refused to take his ideas, like suits, ready-made off the rack. Possessing an original philosophical mind, shaped by a long sojourn in the East and contact with other civilizations, this extraordinary man strongly influenced my own thinking.

When I decided that I would have to broaden my interests if I wished to major in the Romance languages, my stepfather soon let me know that he regarded the matter differently. One day he asked, "Ed, why do you want to study those languages?"

He was a thoughtful man and I recognized at once that he must have carefully weighed his words. "I don't know what you mean," I said.

"You'll have a lot of competition from people who know Spanish and French at least as well as you do. It seems to me you should study some language that is more rare in this part of the world."

I grasped his point but remained puzzled. "What language are you talking about?"

My stepfather lowered his massive dark head, observing me. "Well—for example, Japanese."

"Japanese," I repeated, frowning. "Why Japanese?"

"Ed, Japanese is bound to be one of the languages of the future. The Orient is on the rise, and the two most important countries there are Japan and China. Either this country will go to war with Japan, or Japan will dominate the whole Far East. You're sure to be in demand if you know Japanese."

"I don't know," I said doubtfully.

"Just think about it."

I had deep respect for James Philip Kearney, my stepfather. If he had possessed a flair for publicity and any literary gift, he might have been another T. E. Lawrence, for his life around the time of the First World War was equally adventurous.

Related to Gen. Phil Kearny, the one-armed hero of the Civil War on the Union side, he grew up in New England and became a private investigator early in life. On the eve of the war, he was recruited by M.I.5, the British security service, to take part in the big roundup of suspected German spies residing in England, many of whom falsely claimed U.S. citizenship. Later he joined the British Army and fought in France. After being wounded, he was posted to the Indian Army as a major and commanded a regiment, the Seventy-second Gurkhas, in the Mesopotamian campaign under a tough colonial soldier, Gen. Sir Frederick Stanley Maude, right up to the capture of Baghdad from the Turks. He learned Hindustani (Urdu) and Arabic, becoming proficient in both languages. When tribal warfare broke out on the Northwest Frontier of India after the war, he went there and had many adventures reminiscent of Kipling.

I did not take my stepfather's advice to study Japanese until nearly a year had passed. Then, quite suddenly, I decided to drop my other studies and concentrate on Japanese. The first problem was where to study. Few schools offered Japanese. Columbia University had a course under Hugh Borton, a noted Far Eastern scholar, but once I made up my mind I was in too much of a hurry to wait until I could be accepted for that course.

I stopped by the registrar's office and had a talk with a lady who worked there. She proved to be quite helpful. "Why don't you try the Japanese Buddhist Church?" she said. "It's right here in the neighborhood." She suggested that somebody connected with the church might be willing to teach me.

The idea appealed to me, and one fine spring day I walked over to a street near the university between Broadway and River-side Drive where the Japanese Buddhist Church was located.

It turned out to be an old brownstone house, and I walked slowly up the steps to the front door after looking at the windows and failing to see any sign of life. I rang the bell several times and could hear it pealing inside a seemingly empty house. I looked again at the brass plate beside the door, which bore the name of the church in both English and Japanese script, making certain that I had come to the right place.

Just as I was about to go away, the door opened soundlessly and a slim young Japanese man in a white shirt open at the collar, gray slacks, and sandals peered out at me through a narrow opening.

"I'm looking for someone to teach me Japanese," I said. "I thought that maybe here——"

The young man continued to look at me without expression. I began to wonder whether he had understood. Then he gave a jerky little nod, opening the door wider, and gestured to me to come in.

The hallway was very dim, with a staircase leading into even darker regions above. He took me into another dark, fairly large room that must have once been a parlor. It was now bare except for a couple of chairs, a square table with a bowl of dried flowers, and tall glassed-in cabinets forming a solid mass along one wall until they were broken by a marble mantelpiece above a smoke-blackened fireplace. Sliding oak doors which met in the center closed off another room to the rear, probably the old dining room.

"Wait here," the young man said, pointing toward one of the chairs.

I waited for what seemed a very long time, although it was perhaps no more than ten minutes. Then, quite unexpectedly, an old man, very short, with a deeply seamed face and gray hair, came in from the hall. He must have come from upstairs but I had not heard his footsteps.

The old man had a very shy manner. "I am Hisai," he said in barely audible English. "So you wish to study Japanese?"

That was the beginning of a five-year association with Mr. Hisai—Hisai-san, as he was called in his own language—during which I came to the Buddhist Church twice a week for lessons. Hisai-san always wore plain but decent civilian clothes; I never saw him when he was not neatly dressed in a suit and white shirt with tie. I never learned what he did when he was not teaching me Japanese. I knew nothing of the life he led apart from those times.

It also struck me as curious that I scarcely ever encountered any other person on my visits to that house; at most I would see a man or a couple of men on their way in or out. The place did not in any way correspond to my vision of a Buddhist church. I did not catch sight of robed priests or become aware of the presence of worshippers. If there was an altar with a likeness of the Buddha or a gong or the incense that I associated with Buddhism, I never saw any of it.

In all those years I did not meet Hisai-san on any social occasion; by tacit understanding, it appeared, neither of us attempted to move our relationship from the professional to the social plane. Of course this could be attributed partly to the difference in our ages as well as the cultural gulf that stood between us. I also felt a certain awe before my teacher. Yet the small sums Hisai-san received from me in payment for the lessons seemed to be a welcome addition to his income.

Twice a week I sat with Hisai-san in the room directly above the parlor where I had originally met him. It did not differ in any important detail from the other room, since it contained only the bare minimum of furniture and had exactly the same physical layout. There was nothing of a personal nature to be seen anywhere, and I could only assume that the men who appeared to be the sole inhabitants slept on the upper floors and kept their few personal belongings up there.

Possibly the FBI, which presumably maintained a surveillance of all Japanese institutions in New York at that critical time, was keeping the Buddhist Church under observation, but if so I remained ignorant of it and may have become an object of attention as a frequent visitor without being aware of the fact.

In any case, I knew nothing of any subversive activities in or around the Japanese Buddhist Church. I hardly knew anything about Hisai-san himself except that, by his own account (which I had no reason to doubt), he came from Yokohama.

All that mattered to me at the time was the fact that Hisai-san willingly and industriously did his best to teach me Japanese. Perhaps he also wished to improve his English, which was rudimentary. Whatever his thoughts and interests, he obviously took me at face value and, in a quiet way, appreciated my interest in his native language. Even though my purpose in learning Japanese remained utilitarian, I developed a strong interest in Japan's history and culture. (Unquestionably the French were on the right track in spreading the knowledge of their language throughout the world, for foreigners who became fascinated with the language soon fell under the influence of French culture.) Whatever either of us thought just then, it ultimately emerged that communication is important not only for friends but also for enemies.

Hisai-san's name meant "Ancient Well" and to me he represented exactly that—an ancient font of wisdom, the arcane wisdom of the East. He always remained the wise teacher and I the respectful pupil. The Japanese language that he taught gave me access to that wisdom. I came to admire the Japanese more and more as I gained familiarity with their language and could appreciate their ingenuity in retaining the old forms while adapting the language to the needs of the modern world.

About the third century A.D. the Japanese, having no written language of their own, began to adopt Chinese ideographs and to use them for words of a similar meaning in their spoken language. Each ideograph represented one picture, one idea, one meaning, and hence it was not difficult to apply the ideographs to Japanese words with the same meaning. By the ninth century they also adopted the Chinese pronunciation of that day for compound words made up of several ideographs to express more abstruse or complex meanings. Thus the Japanese applied their own word from the spoken language to a single Chinese ideograph in expressing simple ideas like "man" or "mountain" but kept the Chinese pronunciation for the same ideographs in compound expressions made up of more than one ideograph. Although Chinese pronunciation changed in the course of centuries, the Japanese continued to use the old pronunciation dating from the time when they had taken over those expressions.

This ingenious if cumbersome system, which remained intact until modern times, required a literate Japanese—and practically all Japanese were literate thanks to the excellence of their educational system—to learn a number of different pronunciations or readings, as many as four or five, for the same ideograph, and there were thousands of ideographs in general use. From this point of view, Japanese was more difficult than Chinese, which normally employed only one sound for each ideograph, although Chinese involved the use of far more ideographs.

But the ingenuity of the Japanese in adapting their ancient language to modern requirements did not stop there. They also invented two phonetic alphabets consisting of fifty letters in each case, one—*katakana*—being essentially printing or block letters, and the other—*hiragana*—the equivalent of cursive writing. In this way the Japanese gave themselves the possibility of spelling out words (in syllables) as an alternative to the memorizing of ideographs and their sounds. Unofficial attempts to introduce *rōmaji*, or the Latin alphabet, as a substitute for both Chinese characters and the phonetic alphabet failed in Japan much as similar attempts failed in China.

After teaching me katakana and hiragana, Hisai-san began

working with me using the same first-grade reader bound between tan cardboard covers that could be found in Japanese primary schools. That and more advanced readers had delicate Oriental illustrations in color which I found very pleasing. The first sentence I learned to read in katakana was *Sakura no hana ga saita*—"The cherry blossoms are in bloom."

Over the next five years I went through the grades like a Japanese schoolboy (at a somewhat swifter pace), reader by reader, following the curriculum approved by Japan's Ministry of Education. And in due course I reached the point where I could read newspapers, magazines, and books.

By this time it was becoming obvious to almost anyone who followed current events that war with Japan was very near. Imperial Japan could not or would not be diverted from its expansionist aims in Asia, while the United States, despite preoccupation with the war in Europe, chose to adopt a hard line and followed a policy of open opposition to Japanese expansion. The two powers were headed on a collision course that neither side seemed able to avert.

I had learned all I could from Hisai-san and bade my teacher a warm farewell, presenting him with a leather wallet as a parting gift, although our relations from beginning to end remained businesslike rather than social. Nevertheless, I felt a deep regard for the man, for his modesty and humility, for the kindness that I was sure resided within him, just under the surface.

The barbarism of the Japanese which our servicemen were to encounter during the war and which would leave a permanent residue of bitterness and hatred among many of them reflected a frightening side of the Japanese character. Yet Americans in war showed a callousness and a lack of imagination with regard to human suffering, especially on a larger scale, for example, concerning nuclear or saturation bombing of civilian populations, that hardly reflected well on us.

I had a job in a liquor store in Washington Heights which gave me ample time, when there were no customers, to study Japanese in the back of the store. In the meantime I made inquiries at the local branch of the Office of Naval Intelligence (ONI), and its representative sent me down to the navy recruiting office to take a physical examination.

I was told by a chief petty officer to take off my eyeglasses and read the eye chart, which obviously required 20/20 vision. "I can't read the chart without my glasses," I protested. The CPO was unmoved: "There are plenty who can."

I wrote a letter to the Navy Department in Washington. While I awaited a reply, I went on studying as Japan steadily pursued its southward advance toward Indochina, the Philippines, and the East Indies, pushed deeper into China, and accelerated the Kwantung Army's buildup on the border of the Soviet Union next to Manchuria. Several weeks later, to my surprise, I received a letter inviting me to come to Washington for an interview.

Since everything in Washington seemed novel and strange to me, I kept watching the streets and buildings until the motorman called out the street where I had to transfer to another streetcar bound for my destination, the Navy Building at 18th Street and Constitution Avenue.

There was a loop at Constitution Avenue where the streetcar turned around, and at this point I got off and saw, for the first time, the long, low, gray "temporary" buildings which dated from the First World War. One, the closest, was the Navy Building, and next to it, farther along the avenue in the direction of the Potomac, was the so-called Munitions Building, which then housed the army, for construction of the Pentagon across the river in Virginia had not yet begun.

The tall straight marine, who seemed typical of his kind, on guard inside the doors in the center of the Navy Building ignored me along with the other civilians who were going in and out. Finally I managed to get his attention and obtain directions to the office on the third floor (or third deck, in navy terminology) which I needed to find.

I entered the usual reception room with two secretaries seated at desks facing the door, one of them casting a blank stare at her typewriter as she eased the cover off a cardboard container of coffee. The other secretary, a fragile brunette with a tip-tilted nose, attractively clad in a polka-dot dress, appeared to be interested in the purpose of my visit, and I showed her the letter. She invited me to take a seat by a table piled high with magazines, most of them news weeklies several months out of date. Having been in many reception rooms, I was conditioned to the tedious business of waiting until someone—doctor, dentist, or bureaucrat—decided to deal with me.

I picked up a lonely copy of *Esquire* magazine in which I happened to find an article written by a U.S. Navy admiral. The admiral wrote that if Japan dared to fight the United States, the U.S. Navy would send the Imperial Navy to the bottom within six months.

I had ample time to read the whole article and to ponder the admiral's message. Indeed it sounded as if neither the United States in general nor the U.S. Navy in particular would ever have much need for my services. After the exchange of correspondence, however, I could not very well simply get up and leave, so I resisted the inclination and continued to wait with somewhat dampened enthusiasm.

At last Secretary Number Two, the lively one, answered a buzz and spoke into her telephone for a moment, then got up briskly and led me into another office. I was not so distracted that I failed to note her trim ankles. Once again she invited me to take a seat and left me alone in the room.

The office in which I found myself was large and handsomely furnished as government offices go. It had a number of glass-enclosed cabinets containing leather-bound volumes of U.S. Naval Proceedings, none of which seemed ever to have been opened. There were two desks of the sort commonly called executive in government parlance, both clean of papers, and long tiers of windows taking up a full wall to look out on a depressing view of similar windows in the next wing. Through these windows I could look farther back to see an enclosed bridge that connected the opposite wing with the wing of an identical building in the rear. Two sailors in white summer uniforms were just strolling over the bridge as I looked out, and I admired what I took to be their rolling gait.

I sat there for a while, wondering what I was doing in Washington, in the Navy Department, and asking myself how long it would take before I would be politely but firmly shown the door. Then the door burst open, and a very tall and thin man with white hair and a patrician face, wearing a white shirt with the sleeves rolled up to his elbows, came into the room with soft, quick footsteps. He put me at ease immediately although he seemed shy, for his manner was quiet and businesslike. Wasting no time on preliminaries, he produced a book, selected a page, and asked me to read.

To my relief, I realized at once that I would have no difficulty in reading the book. I learned later that it belonged to the Naganuma series of U.S. Navy textbooks which had been developed for the training of language officers. During the Depression and peacetime years the navy assigned a carefully chosen few of its Annapolis graduates to receive this training in Tokyo. These officers constituted the cream of the crop, but precisely because they were few in number they could not fully meet the navy's wartime requirements. Nevertheless, some of that experience was helpful in planning for the expansion of language training which had become urgent as war approached, although I was as yet scarcely aware of the true situation.

In actuality, however, the man interviewing me was a civilian, not a naval officer. His name, I learned later, was Glen Shaw, and he had achieved a measure of fame in Tokyo, where he had spent many years and obtained the admiring recognition of the Japanese as the Honorable Shaw. He spoke fluent Japanese, having worked as a reporter for one of the principal Tokyo dailies, *Mainichi* or *Asahi Shimbun*. Since I knew nothing at that time about his reputation, I was awed by his obvious knowledge and competence.

Shaw indicated satisfaction as I read various selections that he made, skipping around in the book. He brought the test to a close with a pleasant smile:

"That's enough. I'd like to introduce you to my boss, Commander Hindmarsh."

He took me into an adjoining office where I met a stocky, dark-haired man of medium height dressed in a khaki uniform with shoulder boards bearing the three stripes of a full commander. Albert Hindmarsh had a square face and wore silver-rimmed eyeglasses. Despite the uniform, he looked very professorial, a serious but also humorless sort of man.

Shaw gave Hindmarsh a meaningful glance. Hindmarsh turned to me. "Would you be willing to go up to Harvard University?"

This unexpected proposal caught me by surprise. Before I could think of a reply, Hindmarsh went on: "We have a Japanese language course in Cambridge. Can you be there by a week from this coming Monday?"

Somewhat dazed, I said yes.

I shook hands with both men while Shaw added that if I completed the course successfully I would be commissioned as an ensign in the navy. After absorbing some additional instructions, I went on my way.

I did not delay my return to New York by sightseeing in Washington. I retraced my route by trolley to Union Station, where, looking back over my shoulder from the great entranceway, I caught a glimpse of the Capitol dome looming up in unreal fashion not far away.

As the train rolled northward, I gazed out at the fields and woods, the bays and rivers and inlets of Maryland with evening shadows falling across them.

Although I realized obscurely that I had reached a turning point in my life, I had no idea how greatly my life would be affected or that, before long, millions of other Americans, at this moment completely unaware of what history held in store for them, would be facing the same kind of fateful, possibly fatal, watershed in their lives.

CHAPTER 2

When the Harvard Yard Went to War

JACK Kennedy, who had graduated from Harvard University only a year earlier, in 1940, wrote a book called *Why England Slept*, but another Kennedy, perhaps, could have written with equal validity a book entitled *Why America Slept*.

In that part of Cambridge, Massachusetts, which was peculiar to Harvard, everything that fall seemed perfectly normal. The undergraduates in the various houses went about their pursuits as their predecessors had done for many years before 1941. People walked slowly along the banks of the Charles in autumn sunshine under falling russet leaves while oarsmen navigated the river in a stately, proper manner. As in Washington, the sleepy capital of the nation, no one gave any sign of awareness that the waves that lapped the Atlantic coast on our side of the ocean stretched away to a Europe aflame with war or that the waters running up on the wide beaches of our Pacific coast also touched an Asia reverberating with the sound of battle. Yet for all this appearance of peace in America there were hundreds of thousands of draftees in military

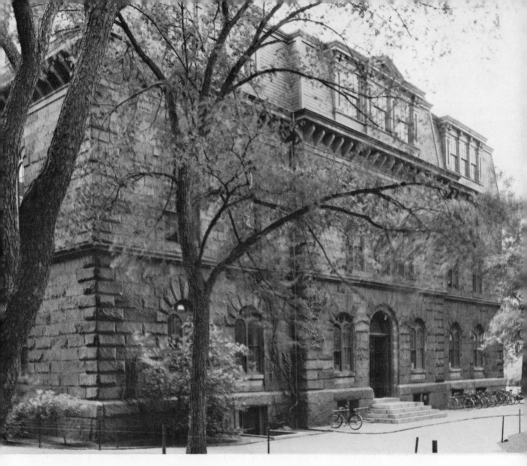

1. Boylston Hall on Harvard University's campus, home of the Yenching Institute and the U.S. Navy's Japanese language school during World War II. *Courtesy of Harvard University.*

camps; the press kept reporting almost daily, it seemed, plane crashes caused by inexperienced military pilots; and that same fall Roosevelt signed into law a record tax bill to pay for our rearmament. Most of us were more concerned with the World Series in which the Yankees, led by the superb Joe DiMaggio, crushed the Brooklyn Dodgers, four games to one.

Even at Yenching Institute, in the tree-shaded Harvard Yard, where our small group had assembled, the U.S. Navy's crash course in the Japanese language attested only superficially to any preparedness on the part of the U.S. government. For the plain truth was that when Washington officially took note of the urgent need for Japanese linguists in this great nation of ours, there were practically none to be had. Not at any rate if one excluded both first- and second-generation ethnic Japanese on account of the security problem. The attitude toward Japanese-Americans in general was exemplified at a later date, after the outbreak of war, by a cartoon in the *New Yorker* that showed a long line of look-alike Nipponese in jungle uniforms, presumably somewhere in Malaya, one of whom was saying, "I wonder if I'll get back my old job in Frisco after the war?"

I learned that in addition to our group at Harvard the navy had recruited another group which was simultaneously going into a similar crash course at the University of California. However, as I became acquainted with the members of our own group, it was obvious that the navy was scraping the bottom of the barrel, or would have been had there been anything in the barrel to begin with.

Some fellow students were missionaries' sons who had been born, and spent their early lives, in Japan. There were others, like Sy Millstein who later became my roommate, who had gone to Japan on business and learned the language in that way. Some had studied Japanese in college. I had studied Japanese in a Buddhist church. Another man, Larry Bukens, had been a New York taxi driver who presumably studied the language in his spare time between fares.

But going farther afield there were others who did not know Japanese at all but were thought to have some facility because they had been in China or had studied Chinese. Some of these people were genuine Chinese scholars and did in fact make the transition into Japanese with relative ease. But this was not always the case. One dreamy young man, a budding poet, had learned some ideographs in order to read Chinese poetry, which held a certain fascination for him. He was recruited for the navy's language program but disappeared one day without leaving a trace. And there was also a man named Siemer, an engineer by profession, who came from Staten Island, where I used to live.

"Hindmarsh contacted me and asked me if I would like to come into the program. I asked him how he had found me and he said that he had consulted an engineers' directory which revealed that I was born in Shanghai. I admitted that that was true but said that I knew no Chinese because my parents had taken me back to the States when I was a year old. I could identify exactly one Chinese character. Hindmarsh told me it didn't matter, they still wanted me. . . ."

Among the "China hands" was one middle-aged man, Jack Robinson, of medium height and solidly built, who had a face that somehow brought to mind the actor Edward G. Robinson (although the similarity in name appeared to be entirely coincidental). Jack Robinson and his plain, unpretentious wife had lived in China for many years, and they were bitterly opposed, so it was said, to Chiang Kai-shek. Since Chiang, like Stalin, had become a democratic ally, it was assumed that Robinson sympathized with Chiang's enemies, the Chinese Communists, and therefore must be a Communist himself. But in 1941 being a Communist was no bar to government service; in some quarters (though not in the navy) it might be considered an asset. Whatever the truth about these matters, Robinson remained a mysterious figure, perhaps for no better reason than that he was so much older than the rest of us and consequently had less in common with us.

On my arrival in Cambridge I went directly to the office in Yenching Institute and met Betsey Dennis, a pert and pleasant blonde, who took charge immediately and, as with other members of the group, saw to it that I got started in the right direction. Betsey, who was married to Reid Dennis, a graduate student, sent me to the Harvard Business School campus where I was assigned to a dormitory room. My roommate, Don Ray, was already fully installed in the room and helped me to get settled. Don came from a family that owned a chain of dry-cleaning stores in Denver, and I, being from a much less affluent background, soon envied him the smart convertible that symbolized his family's resources. I, of course, did not even own a car.

Most of the people in our group were housed in the dormitory, but some, more concerned with privacy and independence, had found rooms off campus in Cambridge.

I learned that I could take my meals in the Business School cafeteria, which was down the street from the dormitory; it was a short walk, and I enjoyed the opportunity to get a bit of air before settling down to study for the remainder of the evening.

Our group of roughly twenty-five was divided into a number of classes on the basis of our knowledge of Japanese. I was placed in the top class and quickly made the acquaintance of the four other students with whom I would be spending the equivalent of an academic year. It would have been very hard to find five more diverse individuals, even in the talents that we brought to our study of Japanese.

Ed Schaefer, dark, intense, very nervous, was something of a genius in his knowledge of Chinese. Even the instructors regarded him with profound respect. Schaefer made phenomenal progress in Japanese on the basis of this erudition. He was a loner who did not appear to make friends easily, and he had a rumpled, untidy look which suggested that he did not bother much about externals.

Another outstanding member of the class was Jack Hall, a graduate of Amherst, who had grown up in Japan and whose father was a missionary. In a sense, he and Ed Schaefer personified the opposing Chinese principles of yang and yin: the golden youth and the black vagabond prince; the one smiling and approachable where the other was somber and forbidding; a slim and easy manner with a touch of the collegiate emphasized by Hall's casual sports jacket with leather patches at the elbows and tweed trousers, set off against the almost studied defiance of Schaefer's thrown-together appearance and aura of an outsider.

Not surprisingly, Jack had learned to speak Japanese as a child, and like those who had been exposed to life in Japan at an early age he had the advantage of an instinctive feeling for both language and culture which others like me lacked and would probably never acquire.

After graduating from Amherst, Jack Hall returned to Japan to teach English at Dōshisha University in Kyoto, the ancient capital, site of the Kinkakuji, the Golden Temple on a lake. Kyoto was filled with moated castles and all that belonged to Japan before its encounter with the crass materialism and cold, impersonal technology of the West. But the city was different in this period because Jack found himself in a country that was already at war. The coal needed for heat was being consumed for other purposes by a voracious war machine, and so, in order to keep warm in winter, Jack went early in the morning to the public bath. By immersing himself in the hot bath, which in Japan is far hotter than elsewhere, he was able to accumulate enough inner warmth to last him through the bitter cold of the day. "The rats refused to eat Japanese soap because it had no glycerine, which was going into explosives," he recalled later. "But when I got hold of a cake of American soap they ate it all without leaving a trace."

Hall left Japan before regular travel between that country and the United States ceased (the time was not far off when the Swedish liner *Gripsholm* had to evacuate Americans from Japan and my old teacher Hisai-san along with other Japanese had to be evacuated from the United States on the same ship). Whatever he had seen of the reverse side of Japan—racism and jingoism—he did not lose faith in the quintessential Japan or, above all, the Japanese people.

Another of my classmates was Ernie Kroll, the only one among us who had already been commissioned as an ensign (there was one other in the whole group, Walter Nichols, who had the same distinction, but he was in a lower class). This seemed strange in a way, for Ernie was a very gentle soul, sensitive to a fault, a poet in an age that rejected poetry, perhaps because it spoke from the heart and our contemporaries distrusted, feared, and were embarrassed by emotion. Kroll had studied Japanese and acquired an excellent command of the language, although I did not learn then or later about his background.

The last of my classmates happened to be the youngest. Dave

2. Edward Van Der Rhoer
in Cambridge in 1941.

Huggins was nineteen or twenty. Unlike the rest of us he had Japanese blood in his veins since his grandfather, the Brinkley who had written a notable history of Japan, had married a Japanese woman and became, as far as I could ascertain, virtually Japanese. Dave himself spoke a fluent and idiomatic Japanese that he had practically learned in the cradle; he was small and swarthy in complexion, with an Oriental shape to his face and eyes, but his looks showed he had mixed blood and he could not have passed for a Japanese. His older brother was a student in the navy program at the University of California. In many ways Dave still seemed more like a child than a potential naval officer.

It took me a little longer to get acquainted with other students in the group, particularly in view of the fact that I followed a very strict schedule of study. After breakfast in the cafeteria I walked over alone to Yenching Institute, where I had most of my classes. On those crisp, sparkling days when autumn leaves were falling, I enjoyed that walk, which took me across the bridge over the Charles and past the red brick houses where undergraduates lived and finally up to Harvard Square and through the wall into the Yard.

When I had finished my classes, I retraced my steps back

across the river to my dormitory room. I sat at my desk and studied the rest of the afternoon until dinner time. I had a "magic slate"—a toy dear to many children—that I found very practical in writing Chinese characters over and over again until the slate was full and I would lift the page to clear the slate and begin anew with my writing.

I liked to work with my table radio on, listening to music, but Don Ray, who had an identical desk against the opposite wall and was trying to concentrate doggedly on his studies, lost patience from time to time and shouted, "Shut that damn thing off!" Since he was having increasing difficulties with his work, I always accepted his protests and did as I was told, but a kind of tug-of-war between us continued—a good example of the way roommates can get on one another's nerves.

I would walk through the dusk of the evening to dinner at the cafeteria, take a short stroll, and go back to my room to study some more until bedtime. Fortunately, both Don and I liked to go to bed at an early hour in order to get a good night's rest, so this particular form of irritation—when one roommate wants to go to bed early and the other has the habit of staying out late—did not trouble our relations.

The next day I resumed the same routine, which continued all week long. The only time I deviated from this routine was on Saturday, when I took time off for some recreation, above all on Saturday night, when I would go into Boston for dinner in a restaurant and possibly a movie or another type of social engagement.

There were times when I ate alone or with a friend in some restaurant like Durgin Park down in the Market, which was famous for its food. Sometimes a group of us accompanied by a few of our teachers and their wives would go to Chinatown, where those who were most experienced in such matters took on the task of ordering a sumptuous Chinese dinner.

However, on Sunday things came back to normal. I slept late, had a larger breakfast than on other days, walked a little along the Charles, and came back to my room, where I read the Sunday newspapers for a while and then resumed my usual routine of study.

Once in a great while I would take a weekend to go to New York, rushing to South Station on Friday night, getting home to our apartment late, often failing to get to bed until three in the morning. I would have a late snack with my mother and stepfather, talk about my own experiences in Cambridge, which they listened to with great interest, enjoy my stepfather's iconoclastic comments about sundry subjects, and read the New York morning papers before falling exhausted into my old bed. On Saturday I would have an opportunity to look up friends or go out with a girl. Then on Sunday afternoon I caught a train at Grand Central and headed back to Boston.

Meanwhile all around Cambridge there was the same appearance of "business as usual." Being so close to the stadium, I managed to see a few football games. Harvard's eleven was not exactly a powerhouse, but after losing its first two games to Pennsylvania and Cornell, the team compiled a respectable record for the rest of the season under coach Dick Harlow, and a guard on that team, Endicott Peabody, was everybody's choice for All-American. One of the games I saw was Harvard's scoreless tie with Navy, when I could not make up my mind which team to root for as a Harvard student and future naval officer.

The young men in crimson mufflers and heavy overcoats and the pretty girls wearing large golden chrysanthemums came to the football games following the traditions of past years. The crowds were not as large perhaps and some of the old enthusiasm was missing, but on the surface nothing had changed that much. And yet *something* had changed.

FDR was having warplanes built in phenomenal numbers and the automobile factories had curtailed their normal production. As men of draft age weighed the advisability of volunteering before they were drafted, automobile dealers showed their usual keen business sense by promising that if you turned in your car before going into the service, you would be among the first to get a new car when the assembly lines started functioning again, presumably after the war. Few people asked themselves how much they could rely on such promises.

Occasionally, to vary my routine of study, I would go out with a girl to dinner and a play, usually one having out-of-town tryouts before reaching Broadway. I also filled the breach when Sy Millstein, who was popular with girls, could not keep a date because he had made last-minute arrangements on behalf of a lady friend from New York to stay at the Hotel Commander in Cambridge over the weekend.

A big man with a nice sense of humor, Sy had played football at Dartmouth (unfortunately acquiring a knee injury) and later soccer in Japan, where he discovered that despite his size he had all he could do to cope with the small but tough Japanese players. Sy gently poked fun at his roommate, Wes Fishel, a little fellow with an eager expression and a quick smile, whom he accused of being a hypochondriac (Fishel had one dresser drawer filled with patent medicines which he gladly offered to anyone who showed up with a sniffle).

Only a few members of our group were married. Among them were Jack Robinson and his wife, who were both well past college age. Then there was Andy Roth, strongly politically motivated, who brought back memories of other students from New York's City College with "causes," and his pretty wife, Renée.

Another married couple were the Hitchcocks—Jim, scarcely seeming old enough to be married, and Babbie, with the emaciated look of a Katharine Hepburn. Hitchcock, who was still another missionary's son born in Japan, had returned to the United States for his education and graduated from Yale. He had forgotten practically all the Japanese he knew as a child, and it was wonderful to see how, little by little, he retrieved this knowledge, even the sounds and cadence of the language, which had been stored away somewhere in his brain.

Apart from the few married men, there were others like Schuyler ("Ki") Cammann and his roommate, Dave Anthony, who both appeared to be teetering on the edge of marriage, since they were going steady with girls at Wellesley and Radcliffe. Anthony, a minister's son who had become known for a booming laugh that seemed to paralyze him at times, was fun to be with, although I felt especially drawn to Ki, who was older and more serious and had an attractive, shy personality. Ki was also a Chinese scholar who had already taken part in an expedition into the Gobi Desert.

The rest of us were largely unattached males, but our demanding study schedules did not allow much time to form lasting attachments to girls if we hoped to keep up with the work.

In our classes we were rotated from one teacher to the other in order to give us maximum exposure to different degrees of knowledge and style.

First and foremost, of course, was a wonderful Russian, Professor Serge Elisséeff, the head of Yenching Institute. He had led a life that was more fascinating than many to be found in works of fiction, and he would have been an equally fascinating subject for a book based on his own life.

To Americans, Russians always appear colorful, and Elisséeff was certainly no exception. He was a short, rotund man with a round cherubic face that was perpetually smiling and intelligent eyes hidden behind thick glasses. When he taught, he drew upon a rich fund of stories, most of them personal and each with a humorous point that reflected his ability to laugh at himself as well as others.

Elisséeff's career as a leading Japanese scholar began when he was already living in Japan, well before the First World War. Elisséeff, who boasted that he had owned the first motorcycle in Tokyo, liked to tell the story of the time he was chugging at ten miles an hour down a narrow street when a peddler on a bicycle suddenly emerged from a side street in front of him. Unfortunately, as was customary in those days, the peddler was carrying his wares on a long bamboo pole that he balanced on his shoulders as he rode along. The encounter was so unexpected for both parties that a collision could not be avoided; Elisséeff ran with his motorcycle head-on into the peddler, throwing the man off his bicycle and scattering his wares far and wide. The wails of the peddler attracted a crowd, as usual in Japan, in a space of time that seemed like seconds. At almost the same moment Elisséeff caught sight of a policeman in the distance who was rapidly approaching. Elisséeff knew the reputation of Tokyo's Metropolitan Police Department, which in those days was justly noted for its toughness and for the alacrity with which it cracked down on foreigners who violated the laws of the country. Without further delay Elisséeff quickly crammed the contents of his pockets, a number of crumpled bills, into the peddler's hands and then sped off on his motorcycle.

As they both knew at once, the amount of money he had given the peddler greatly exceeded the value of the wares, so, to Elisséeff's amusement then and later, the peddler accompanied his departure with deep bows and a repeated "*Maido arigatō gozaimasu*," which was the Japanese shopkeeper's normal way of saying, "Thank you, come again."

After the Bolsheviks seized power in Russia in October 1917 (November, according to the present calendar), ruthless reprisals soon began against the Bolsheviks' "class" enemies, primarily the bourgeoisie, although this was interpreted fairly liberally, one might say, to include all of their political foes such as Socialist, non-Communist workers and peasants hostile to the Bolshevik cause. There was no question, however, about Serge Elisséeff because his family had long been prominent in Petrograd as owners of the well-known Elisséeff gourmet store in that city. When he was arrested, the Bolsheviks were inclined to shoot him. According to his own story, which might have been apocryphal, he told the Bolsheviks: "If you shoot me, you'll kill Russia's greatest living expert on the Japanese language!"

Supposedly this admonition gave the Bolsheviks pause, since they were only too well aware that Russia had fought a losing war against Japan in 1904–5 and might have to fight the Japanese again. In any event, they spared Elisséeff's life at that time. He waited until he could safely cross the border and escape from Russia, making his way to France, where he lived for some years before coming to the United States.

Elisséeff was not only a stimulating teacher but also a great raconteur and pleasant companion. He never adopted the aloof behavior toward his students characteristic of some professors puffed up with their own importance and yet suffering from insecurity.

One afternoon I was visiting some fellow students in a rooming house off Harvard Square. It was a beautiful, sunny day, and since the weather had not yet turned cold I had taken up a position on the windowsill of their room overlooking the street. I was sitting half in and half out of the window. Suddenly I became aware of Professor Elisséeff's well-rounded figure ambling like an amiable bear in our direction.

I called out his name. Elisséeff stopped dead in his tracks and looked up. Then I waved at him. He saw me in the window, waved back, and without hesitation turned in at the walk and climbed up the stairs to the porch. I warned the others, and we all listened to the creaking of his footsteps on the stairs. Since the door was also open, he easily found his way to the room, where we gave him a warm if bemused welcome.

Someone dredged up a bottle of red wine and found some cheese and crackers in another room, and for the next two hours we enjoyed a lively conversation with the professor, who drank the wine from a water glass (formerly a jelly jar), sniffing its bouquet with obvious appreciation. We managed to cover a wide range of subjects before the professor decided that it was time to go; none of us had dared to interrupt the discourse and express a desire to leave, although we were happy to stay and talk, without any sense of obligation.

The second-ranking man in Yenching Institute was another distinguished academician, despite the fact that he was considerably younger than Elisséeff. Professor Edwin Reischauer had already achieved renown as a scholar, but he had much in common with members of our group, for he was also the son of a missionary and had been born in Japan.

Still slender and youthful in appearance, Ed Reischauer easily won and held our respect with an informal and modest manner combined with unquestionable erudition. He had a ready smile and dark hair slightly touched with gray, cut short in the style then common among college students. His brother Bob, who had also had a promising academic career ahead of him, was killed in the Japanese bombing of Shanghai in 1937. Nevertheless Ed Reischauer, abhorring Japanese militarism as he did, remained unshaken in his deep love of the Japanese people he had known all his life.

Reischauer was the driving force and chief organizer of the navy program at Harvard. He had the help of a competent staff, including Betsey Dennis, who took care of most of the day-to-day problems of the students and provided a shoulder to cry on.

Our other teachers presented fascinating contrasts in origin, background, and experience. One of them was a man named Mackenzie, a bluff, hearty Canadian of Scottish origin who looked as if he had been born in tweeds and to some might have appeared to be the incarnation of Colonel Blimp, although he was definitely no fool. He had lived for many years in Japan and possessed an enviable knowledge of both Japanese speech and mentality.

He constantly extolled the virtues of Nojiri, a mountain resort that he had helped to establish. Despite his panegyrics, Nojiri hardly rivaled the number-one resort, Karuizawa, to which most of Tokyo's society and the diplomatic corps fled when the heat of summer arrived. Karuizawa had a golf course and tennis courts and just about everything else. Nojiri, situated in forest country on a lake, offered more rustic charms that appealed mostly to foreign missionaries and their families whose means were modest and who did not mind "roughing it."

Another excellent teacher of a different sort was Takehiko Yoshihashi, a Nisei (native American citizen), who was a natty dresser, usually carried a briefcase, and maintained a rather formal manner. Despite his reticence, he was popular with the students. Later in Australia during the war, Sy Millstein would see a man in an American army uniform who bore an uncanny resemblance to our Harvard instructor. Jokingly Millstein said, "Hello, Yoshiha-shi!" and the soldier answered to that name, which, it is true, was about as common among Japanese names as Jones would be to Anglo-Saxons. However, this Yoshihashi turned out to be a brother of our instructor. We held him in high regard because he was a serious man who did not intend to waste our time or his.

The staff of teachers would not have been complete without a woman, and in our case this was McKinnon-san, who looked and acted like a typical Japanese girl, which she really was by education and upbringing. But she had an American father and possessed U.S. citizenship, so the circumstances of international life had cast her in the unexpected role of teaching Americans who were to become Japanese language officers in the U.S. Navy.

McKinnon-san was easily embarrassed, like most Japanese women, but if anyone had doubt about her competence as a teacher it was quickly dispelled, and she proved to be invaluable in accustoming us to female voice and speech patterns. She was also very pretty, although her walk aroused mild amusement among the students. They called it the "Tokyo shuffle" because she had not yet shaken off the habit, acquired from many years of wearing clogs, *geta,* and *zōri* (straw sandals), of sliding her feet in a long glide over the ground instead of lifting them at each step.

Gradually we became so immersed in our studies that one day dissolved imperceptibly into the next, the weeks ran together, and the months seemed to slip by unnoticed.

Preoccupied as I was with my own work, I still had time occasionally to drop in on some of the other people in the program. Now and then I visited Siemer, the engineer, who also came from Staten Island and had heard of my father. He had long since given up any effort to study the Japanese language, which was beyond his capacity, and was marking time by playing chess. He was a serious chess player, well schooled in tournament play, and liked to entice me into a game, when he would demolish me in short order. Since I knew nothing of the finer points of the game, Siemer played with

3. Classmates Dave Huggins (left) and Jack Hall and "McKinnon-san," one of the navy's Japanese language teachers.

me like a cat with a mouse, and I soon became discouraged about taking him on as an opponent.

Siemer's roommate, Curt Manchester, was a gentle, professorial person who appeared oddly mismatched with a down-to-earth man like Siemer but was devoted to him, and the two were inseparable during this period.

One Sunday morning I went out for a late breakfast and had my usual stroll before returning to my dormitory room. It was a lovely day with ample sunshine and I enjoyed the brisk air during my walk along the Charles, passing in the shadow of the stadium. When I came back, I could hear the radios turned on in other rooms, their volume set unusually high. I sensed that something out of the ordinary must have occurred. I entered my room and turned on the radio at once, learning for the first time that the Japanese had attacked Pearl Harbor. So it was war . . .

The next day we listened to President Roosevelt as he asked Congress for a declaration of war. Speaking in a ringing voice, he said, "Yesterday, December 7, 1941—a date which will live in infamy—the United States of America was suddenly and deliberately attacked by naval and air forces of the Empire of Japan."

The extent of the disaster that had overtaken us did not become clear at once. We finally learned with dismay and shock about our losses: eight battleships either sunk or put out of action, hundreds of planes destroyed on the ground, several thousand men killed in less than two hours. The Pacific Fleet had virtually ceased to exist for the time being. There was only one bright spot in the picture: the carrier force had been at sea and therefore escaped unscathed.

Before the week was out, the members of our group had been rushed down to the Boston Navy Yard for formal induction into the navy. Despite the seriousness of the occasion, this event also had its comic side. The medical staff that had to deal with us found themselves confronted with some weird birds.

Practically the only one who passed the physical with flying colors was our hypochondriac, Wes Fishel, who was on the verge of flunking out of the course. All the others required waivers, even Fishel's roommate, the former football player Sy Millstein, who made Fishel look like a puny midget.

The doctors threw up their hands at our antics. "Killer" Kane, a frail, overage sort who had been in one graduate school after another for years, questioned whether he had any physical disability. An embarrassing scene occurred when Bill Black, who had been an artist in Paris, was informed that he was color-blind. He flew into a terrible rage, shouting: "That's impossible. I'm an artist! There's no way I can be color-blind."

Once we had been inducted, we went back to the routine of study, hardly noticing the bad news that kept coming in during December and the early part of 1942 as the Japanese occupied Malaya and Singapore, the supposedly impregnable British bastion, destroyed U.S. forces in the Philippines except for the remnants still holding out on Bataan, and quickly shattered the weak Dutch, British, and American naval units in the area of the Dutch East Indies.

All around us other students were getting ready to go to war. In the Business School our neighbors started angling for commissions, aiming for the U.S. Navy Quartermaster Corps as a first

choice. Uniforms of all the services became more and more numerous on the campus.

I took advantage of brief respites from study to go ice skating
for miles along the Charles River, which was completely frozen
over. I came back from these outings with new vigor, my brain
cleared by the biting, crystal-clear air. Then I threw myself eagerly
back into the work.

Now and then I had a little time to read for entertainment.
One of the books that I read with pleasure was Arthur Waley's
translation of a Japanese classic, *Genji Monogatari* or *The Tale of
Genji*.

Another book that was passed from hand to hand within our
group was *The Honorable Picnic*, a satire written by a Frenchman,
Thomas Raucat. The plot centered on a foreigner's attempt to se-
duce a young Japanese girl, and the author used this as an occasion
to make fun of Japanese folkways, portraying them as quaint,
comic-opera types, but at the same time showing foreigners as the
boors Japanese consider them to be.

A slightly erotic note is struck when the Japanese girl who is
the heroine of the story goes to a movie with a friend and, unable
to find a comfortable position in the theater, accepts her friend's
suggestion to sit half on a bench and half on his lap.

"Hardly had I closed my eyes, the better to hear, when I
seemed to feel that the mind of my honorable-friend was not entirely on the movie. I waited a little while. My friend did not let
on, but it was quite true. What a comical incident! As if I would
ever have imagined anything like that!

"Presently I turned my head a little and looked at him smiling
faintly with one eye and a corner of my mouth. That was by way of
indicating that I was not angry and he understood it at once."

The Honorable Picnic was first published in France in 1924,
but even the Japanese of that day could not have been quite as
quaint and amusing as they are portrayed, although the author
does point correctly to certain customs that Westerners often laugh
at. However, the Japanese were only too well acquainted with

harsh reality. The year before the book was published, in 1923, about ninety-one thousand people died as a result of an earthquake and the fires that followed it, destroying one-third of Tokyo and the whole of the neighboring city of Yokohama. For us, in the year 1942, it was clear that the Japanese who had built the formidable war machine that we saw in action in the thirties did not come out of *Madame Butterfly*.

In April we heard the first encouraging news from the Pacific theater when U.S. bombers commanded by Lt. Col. Jimmy Doolittle carried out an astonishing raid on Tokyo—astonishing to Americans who had not expected that we would be able to strike at the heart of the enemy so soon and to the Japanese who were suddenly sobered by the realization that their great successes in the war thus far had failed to protect them at home.

Joseph Clark Grew, the American ambassador to Japan, still under internment after the outbreak of war, wrote in his diary on that day (April 18, 1942):

> The Swiss Minister came again, and just as he was leaving before lunch we heard a lot of planes overhead and saw five or six large fires burning in different directions with great volumes of smoke. At first we thought that it was only maneuvers but soon became aware that it was the first big raid on Japan by American bombers which are reported to have attacked first in the Hokkaido and then, in turn, Tokyo, Yokosuka, Nagoya, and Kobe. We saw one of them, apparently losing altitude and flying very low, just over the tops of the buildings to the west, and at first we feared that it had crashed but then realized that it was intentionally following these tactics in order to avoid the dives of pursuit planes and the antiaircraft fire. . . .
>
> The Japanese press claimed that nine enemy planes had crashed, but we doubt if any were lost since, if even one had crashed on land, the papers would have been full of triumphant pictures of the wreck. They appeared too large to have come from an aircraft carrier, and they may have been flying from the Aleutian Islands to the

new air bases in China. We were all very happy and proud in the Embassy, and the British told us later that they drank toasts all day to the American fliers.

When asked where the planes had come from, FDR replied with tongue in cheek, "Shangri-La." Although he was referring to the mythical Asian land described in James Hilton's *Lost Horizon,* he wished to suggest jokingly that we had an air base in the Himalayas. Thus the president sought to maintain military security. We were as much in the dark as the public at large. It turned out, however, that Ambassador Grew was mistaken: while the planes appeared to be too large to have come from an aircraft carrier, this was exactly where they had come from. The raiding force consisted of sixteen B-25 bombers, land-based planes, that had been specially adapted to take off from the flight deck of the carrier *Hornet.* They were launched at a distance of nearly seven hundred miles from Tokyo. Since there was no question of returning to the carrier, the planes flew over Japan, dropped their bombs, and headed for China. As Ambassador Grew had surmised, none of the planes was downed over Japan.

On our side those in positions of authority knew that the raid would have little military significance, but they deemed it worthwhile for the psychological boost it would give to the American people. But the very mystery of the origin of the planes had an effect on the war that no one could have anticipated at the time. There were influential people in the Japanese Navy's high command who favored Australia and India as the next targets, but Yamamoto, who still wished to complete the destruction of the U.S. Navy, asserted that the planes in the Tokyo raid must have come from Midway and therefore the Imperial Navy had to turn eastward and capture Midway and the western Aleutians.

High strategy did not concern me and the members of our group at that time. News that was far more electrifying came soon after, when the five members of our class—Schaefer, Hall, Kroll,

Huggins, and I—received orders to proceed to Washington without delay. Although we still had not completed our studies, someone on the top level had evidently decided that our services were needed for the war effort right now.

Curiously enough, while we had continued our studies at Harvard essentially undisturbed, the navy's other group at the University of California had been forced to move to the University of Colorado at Boulder. This occurred because of the mass evacuation of Japanese from the West Coast and their internment on orders of our government. Since a number of teachers in that course were Nisei and given the negative public attitude to all things Japanese at that time, it proved to be impossible to continue studies of this sort in California.

The whole problem had been precipitated after the Japanese attack on Pearl Harbor by panic on the part of both the authorities in California, who feared a possible fifth column among the numerous ethnic Japanese there, and the population in general, who reacted with fear and xenophobia against the Japanese, many of them Nisei.

I was appalled at the shameful treatment of these people, who were almost all honorable and law-abiding and whose constitutional rights were being grossly violated; they not only suffered great bodily hardships but lost many of their worldly goods as a result of this unjust action. I was reminded of this almost daily when we were taught by Yoshihashi, who behaved with exemplary dignity and always gave his best efforts, in spite of the fact that his own parents were interned at that time in a camp in Colorado.

In spite of everything we all were caught up in the war, and I packed my belongings with a pang, looking around my dormitory room for the last time. Harvard's *Veritas* seal on the chairs somehow left an indelible image on my memory. Yet I was excited by the unknown future that lay ahead, and this expectation took some of the sting out of leave-taking.

I shook hands warmly with my roommate, Don Ray, wishing him well, but I saw in his eyes another kind of regret—the disappointment of seeing others reach a cherished goal and go on, while, it seemed, he was destined to fail in the language course that he had struggled so hard to master.

"Good-bye, Don," I said. "I'll be seeing you in Washington."

"Sure," he said.

CHAPTER 3

Climb the Highest Mountain

J UST before the surprise attack on Pearl Harbor—while U.S. Naval Intelligence was deceived into the belief that Japanese aircraft carriers were at home in the Inland Sea, in no position to do any harm—Admiral Yamamoto had arranged for the strike force to rendezvous under radio silence far to the north. Japan's unannounced deadline for an understanding with the United States had expired, and in accordance with Yamamoto's orders the strike force of six carriers—*Hiryu, Soryu, Akagi, Kaga, Shokaku,* and *Zuikaku*—with escort ships, was already at sea, headed for Hawaii.

On December 2, 1941, this force received a coded message: "Climb Mount Niitaka." It was a prearranged signal from Yamamoto to proceed with the attack as planned.

Mount Niitaka was a peak on Taiwan whose elevation of nearly 13,000 feet made it the highest point of the Japanese Empire (Mount Fuji, 12,395 feet high, owed its fame chiefly to its beautiful conical shape and its isolated situation on the approaches to Tokyo). The symbolism of the reference to Mount Niitaka was clear: the

4. The author and his stepfather,
James Philip Kearney.

decision to go to war had been made. The strike force was to deliver the first blow at Pearl Harbor and put the U.S. Pacific Fleet out of action.

Although in keeping with the symbol the Japanese had, by their devastating attack on Pearl Harbor, successfully climbed the highest mountain, in the months that followed they had to make a descent from this peak, where they could not remain indefinitely.

Jack Hall, Ed Schaefer, and I knew little about what was happening in the Pacific when we followed orders and reported to Washington in the spring of 1942. Our immediate concerns loomed larger: to be fitted for uniforms, to complete a series of inoculations, and to find temporary housing in a city that was already beginning to bulge at the seams.

We managed to find a large front room with three beds in a rooming house just off Columbia Road. It was not a particularly auspicious period of cohabitation, as all three of us were feverish and had sore arms from typhoid inoculations. Moreover, Jack Hall and I discovered that Ed Schaefer had one particularly annoying habit that robbed us of sleep every night. Ed would go out to a rental library and come back with four or five mystery novels that he proceeded to devour by staying awake all night to read. The single electric light hanging from the ceiling stayed lit throughout the long night. I buried my head under the pillow but did not succeed in getting much sleep, so our nights turned out to be one interminable agony.

Fortunately, we were not destined to live together very long. Both Ed Schaefer and Jack Hall already had marriage plans. Ed found a place of his own near the Capitol. Jack located a pleasant room in a private house just off 16th Street in what was called the "third alphabet," which meant that it was a considerable distance uptown. Jack planned to live there after he married his fiancée, Robin. He invited me to share the room with him until the wedding took place. I accepted without hesitation, since I liked him and enjoyed his company.

We moved into the house, where the family treated the two young naval officers with great kindness and made us very much at home. Jack brought his collection of Brahms records with him, and we spent much of our spare time listening to the great master's solemn, moving music.

In the Navy Department I was assigned to the Office of Naval Communications and reported for duty in the sixth wing on the first deck.

The office in which I found myself was OP-20-GZ, whose essential function was to recover Japanese codes. No one bothered to explain this top-secret activity to me at the outset. This may have been one of the reasons why the security of the operation was so good; knowledge was confined to those who needed it. In any case, I learned about it only gradually.

No one thought it necessary, either, to show me the Table of Organization and tell me which box I was in, so I only learned about such matters over a long period of time. The Office of Naval Communications, headed by an admiral, was directly subordinate to the chief of naval operations, Adm. Ernest King, a tall bald eagle of a man, whom I occasionally encountered in the passages. Each time I saw him I was glad that I had nothing directly to do with him, not because of his august position but because he looked like the sort who not only "chewed out" people but ate them whole.

OP-20-G, I found out in time, was the part of Naval Communications that had primary responsibility for the U.S. Navy's cryptography and cryptanalysis; in other words, it was responsible for the navy's own codes as well as the breaking of foreign codes.

OP-20-GX handled interception and direction finding, including traffic analysis. Once the initial breakthroughs into Japanese codes and ciphers had been made by the cryptanalysts of OP-20-GY, the responsibility for identifying and recovering code groups with a view to actually reading a code was turned over to my branch, OP-20-GZ, which also made complete or partial translations of the messages based on their importance and the stage of recovery.

When I reported for duty, the boss of OP-20-GZ was an awesome personality, Comdr. Redfield ("Rosey") Mason. I had hardly found a place to sit in the long room filled with shelves and tables on which piles of IBM "runs" lay open for reference purposes when I became very much aware of his presence.

"Christ in the foothills!" shouted the balding, cherubic-faced man seated at one end of the room with his back to the rest of us. He suddenly looked around with a glare. "Where's the latest run that came from the machine room this morning?"

The effect was electrifying. Much scurrying about until someone found the missing volume; the volume itself, however inanimate, managed to look guilty. I was briefly introduced to Commander Mason, who hardly glanced at me, merely grunted, and then said something incomprehensible (at least as far as I was concerned) to Lt. Francis M. Brotherhood, USNR, who had been placed in nominal charge of the new officers.

I was assigned to work with a civilian, a tall, pleasant-faced, rather handsome and distinguished man who had been a curator of Japanese art at the Boston Museum of Fine Arts. Robert Treat Paine, a descendant of the signer of the Constitution of the same name, was everything that the term "proper Bostonian" implied. First and foremost, he was a gentleman, a person of breeding, a man of dignity, and, obviously, of good education. He was a graduate of Harvard and had his home in Cambridge, and now as a patriotic duty he had come to Washington to make a contribution where he could be most valuable.

Bob and I became better acquainted at lunch that day. Although he was my senior by at least a dozen years, he behaved toward me in such a natural and appealing way that I liked and respected him from the beginning.

When I mentioned Mason, Bob said: "Oh, dear. Well, how do you think I felt on my first day? I was sitting in a chair right behind him. Obviously he mustn't have known I was there because he suddenly shoved his chair back and crashed into mine, and he started swearing in such a loud voice that I almost fell off."

Rosey Mason was a driving leader who did not spare himself or others. I often had the feeling that he was a candidate for an early ulcer. According to office legend, he had started as a newsboy in Ohio; he was either an orphan or had come from a very poor family. His qualities of leadership were recognized at an early point in his life by people influential enough to help him. He received an appointment to Annapolis and, after graduation, was one of the chosen few sent to Tokyo to study Japanese.

Mason's predecessor as head of OP-20-GZ, Comdr. Alvin D. Kramer, sat at a desk in the corner across from me. He had been relieved of any active participation in the work of the branch. He did not in fact seem to have any particular duties, and, among those who worked there, an understanding hung in the air that Kramer had failed. He was associated with the debacle of Pearl Harbor in his handling of the product of OP-20-GZ, just as on the top level Adm. Harold Stark had been replaced as chief of naval operations, for Pearl Harbor was viewed primarily as a defeat for the U.S. Navy.

I could not help observing Kramer, and I saw him as a broken man. I did not know the extent to which he had been drawn into

5. Commander Redfield ("Rosey") Mason, head of OP-20-GZ.

the work of the Roberts Commission making a preliminary investigation of Pearl Harbor, but it seemed to me that he was involved more in postmortems of that disaster than in anything of current interest.

Most of my colleagues preferred not to speak about Kramer. One bright young yeoman put it into words one day when he mentioned Kramer and said, "He'll never make admiral." This was tantamount to saying that Kramer did not have much of a future in the navy, and even though others did not speak of it the yeoman's evaluation remained the general consensus.

Kramer was a handsome, erect man with brown wavy hair and a moustache. He spoke courteously and in low key to everyone, regardless of rank. He was a gentleman and a scholar of the type produced by the service academies, which produced more roughnecks and antiintellectuals. He would have made an excellent naval attaché moving in diplomatic circles abroad. Yet he differed in some intangible manner from Bob Paine's sort of gentleman and scholar who had acquired the polish from birth as well as education.

In contrast, Mason could best be described as a rough diamond. He was a man you would not want to encounter in a brawl in an alley. Six times a day he sent chills down your spine when he bellowed "Coffee!" at the top of his voice and a chief yeoman came running with the coffee pot. Mason consciously used fear to keep people under control, but it worked. He meant to be a winner, and he was.

Yet he treated Kramer, as far as I could see, with compassion. Perhaps it was a part of the code that made Annapolis men stand together, although that could be stretched only so far, as the unfortunate Admiral Kimmel, who commanded at Pearl Harbor, was finding out. But Mason also realized, in all probability, that the other man was near the limit of physical if not emotional exhaustion. I had no way of knowing whether he ever told himself, in the words of John Bradford, "There but for the grace of God go I. . . ." Kramer fell asleep at his desk day after day. It was said that he often worked late into the night, but no one suggested what he had been doing.

Most of the old-timers in OP-20-GZ were civilians. One man with whom I became friendly at the outset was Ralph Cory, who had done consular work in Japan before the war. He was of medium height, solidly built, with a plain but agreeable face. A taciturn man, he had a simple manner and made no effort to impress others. When I learned that he was already planning to leave, I felt somehow saddened.

We were taking a walk on Constitution Avenue during the lunch break. It was one of those Washington days in early spring which promised that the forsythia bushes would sprout yellow blossoms and the jonquils would push their golden heads up through fresh green lawns at any moment. We walked for a while without speaking, just taking deep breaths of the soft air. Suddenly Cory said, "I'm going into the marines."

"You are?" I said, surprised. "I'm sorry. Why do you want to leave?"

He grimaced. "I'm sick of pencil pushing."

Aside from Cory, some of my other colleagues had Japanese blood, which seemed to make them extremely sensitive to the way they were treated by other people.

Phil Cate, who always reminded me of a kind of inquisitive and very wise bird, was small and slight, the spring of a boy in his step, with an upswept wave of white hair in marked contrast to his dark complexion. His eyes, fluid and deep brown, were his most remarkable feature. Phil had unorthodox ideas about most things, including the raising of children, who, he believed, would be better off without the interference of adults. Ever one to practice what he preached, Phil and his wife allowed their young daughter to manage her own upbringing, which led to a number of complications, some amusing, some irritating, with their less broad-minded neighbors.

Phil's best friend in OP-20-GZ also had some Japanese blood. Fred Woodruff was tall and rather good-looking in a Latin way. He never took the trouble to hide a certain cynicism and often fell into black moods, when he would behave badly. For all that, he was an able and conscientious worker and remained unobtrusive—a quality to be valued in a group of people whose work called for a maximum of concentration.

Fred Woodruff's sister, Mrs. Dorothy Edgers, was fortyish,

still attractive, and chic. She possessed her brother's Latin looks but was smaller, with a nice figure. She had worked as a buyer for a department store in San Francisco. She had been educated in Japan and was qualified to teach in Japanese schools, so her knowledge of the Japanese language was in many respects superior to that of the others. Like her brother, she was very quiet and went about her work with little fuss and much efficiency.

From these people who had lived through the whole period of OP-20-GZ's Pearl Harbor trauma I learned a great deal about what had happened at that time and why it happened.

A little over a year before Pearl Harbor, the United States Navy and Army cryptanalysts had achieved a great triumph: they had managed to reconstruct Imperial Japan's supposedly impregnable Type No. 97 cipher machine. The reconstructed machine received the cryptonym PURPLE from the Americans.

The idea of a cipher machine had exerted an irresistible attraction for cryptographers for many years. Cipher machines could complicate the encipherment of plain text by performing innumerable enciphering operations easily and with great speed, thereby making the work of enemy cryptanalysts enormously difficult. The most ingenious ciphers ever devised by the human brain were limited by the capacity of most men to handle cipher operations both accurately and speedily. A machine did not suffer from such limitations. Ideally, it could devise a completely new cipher for each letter of plain text. Depending on the construction of a language, if the letter z appeared fifteen times in a row in the enciphered text, it could theoretically be deciphered as a different letter of the alphabet every time. Conversely, the letter z could conceivably be enciphered with fifteen different letters of the alphabet in the same message.

The first true cipher machines made their appearance in several countries following the First World War. Although the machines were constructed in different ways, they were based on the same principle: using an elaborate series of rotors, wheels, bars, and lugs to encipher plain text letters according to the irregular movements of devices built into the machine.

One of the first cipher machines to appear on the scene was invented and patented by an American named Hebern in 1921. After many vicissitudes and ups and downs, a modernized version of Hebern's machine was adopted for use by the United States in top-secret communications during World War II.

During the war the United States also made extensive use of another machine, the Hagelin, named for its Swedish inventor. The Hagelin machine was esteemed for its compact size and great durability which allowed it to be used under the most adverse conditions. Later Hagelin transferred his plant to Switzerland, where it turned out machines for many other countries.

A third machine, originally patented by a man named Koch in Holland after the First World War, was acquired by a German, Arthur Scherbius, who lived in Berlin. Scherbius called his new machine ENIGMA, and as the German war effort got under way ENIGMA became the top cryptographic system used by the German armed forces.

Before long the Imperial Navy adapted a cipher machine of its own from ENIGMA, and when this machine was loaned to the Foreign Ministry it underwent further modifications. The Foreign Ministry's machine was named Type No. 97 for the year of its development, abbreviated to '97 from 2597 of the Japanese calendar (using a chronology dating from 660 B.C., the supposed year of accession of the first human emperor of Japan, Jimmu Tennō), which corresponded to 1937.

PURPLE—as the Americans called it—was, however, no mere copy of ENIGMA. The Japanese introduced improvements that made their machine far more complex than the German prototype (and far more of a challenge to enemy cryptanalysts). It consisted of two electric typewriters connected to a box containing the cryptographic elements in a series of relays within an intricate network of wiring. The typewriters provided the initial electrical impulses for enciphering and deciphering, simultaneously recording both plain and cipher text.

The intricacy of the Type No. 97 machine was an unwelcome surprise to those cryptanalysts who attempted to break it. The Japanese had a reputation as expert copiers; manufacturers in the rest of the world took great pains to prevent the Japanese from copying their product. But this did great injustice to the Japanese, who were far more original than their detractors conceded.

Japanese experts were confident that their machine posed insurmountable problems for enemy cryptanalysts. They had good reason to think so. After many months of analysis and study marked by nervous strain and frustration, the American cryptanalysts were almost ready to agree. They had utilized all the statistical knowledge, group theory, and mathematical formulas devised in solving other machine ciphers without really penetrating the secret of the Type No. 97 machine.

Nevertheless, a breakthrough finally came about through an inspired guess by one cryptanalyst who made the kind of leap often required in the realm of thought to cross an abyss. The PURPLE machine built by the Americans even proved to be superior in certain ways to the Type No. 97 machine.

A limited number of PURPLE machines were built and placed in key U.S. installations. Strangely enough, one U.S. installation that never received a PURPLE machine was Pearl Harbor, and this lapse, as it turned out, was to have fateful consequences; had Admiral Kimmel, for example, actually seen the dispatches exchanged between the Japanese in Tokyo and Washington, he might not have allowed himself to be lulled into a false sense of security.

In retrospect, it appeared that the access PURPLE gave us to sensitive Japanese communications prior to Pearl Harbor did more harm than good. The breakthrough that made it possible to read Japan's most important and sensitive diplomatic communications—those passing back and forth between the minister of foreign affairs in Tokyo and the ambassadors in world capitals like Washington, London, Berlin, Rome, and Moscow—had an intoxicating effect on the American inner circle given access to material from the PURPLE machine. Special security measures were taken to guard the secret. The intercepted messages were referred to by the collective name "Magic," and only a select group, which included the president and his closest advisers in the White House, Secretary of State Hull and ranking Foreign Service officers, Navy Secretary Frank Knox, and Secretary of War Henry L. Stimson, as well as the services' top brass, had the opportunity to read some—not necessarily all—of the messages. Magic also had an intoxicating effect on those directly involved in deciphering and translating the messages, a task shared by the Signal Intelligence Service of the army (SIS) and OP-20-G of the navy. Commander Kramer, head of OP-20-GZ at the time, kept one foot in ONI and was himself involved in distributing Magic to people with a "need to know" in the higher echelons.

The fascination with PURPLE, however, had the effect in OP-20-GZ of diminishing interest in other communications intelligence that might have been very useful at the time. Vital clues could turn up in ostensibly unimportant correspondence, as many experienced intelligence officers finally learned in the course of a lifetime: in military terms, more significant information could sometimes be learned from a sergeant than a general. As it happened, the only clue to an imminent attack on Pearl Harbor did not come in high-level diplomatic traffic carried by the Type No. 97 machine. The reason was simple, although we failed to appreciate it then: the Japanese military trusted their diplomats even less than the U.S. military was inclined to trust ours.

Curiously, Ambassador Grew in Tokyo received disturbing information about a possible Pearl Harbor attack as early as January 1941. His informant was the Peruvian minister to Japan, Ricardo Rivera-Schreiber, who deduced from a Japanese interpreter's drunken boast at a diplomatic party, "The American fleet will disappear," that there would be an attack on Pearl Harbor.

Grew immediately reported this information to Washington. (Grew noted in his diary on January 27, 1941: "There is a lot of talk around town to the effect that the Japanese, in case of a break with the United States, are planning to go all out in a surprise mass attack on Pearl Harbor. . . .") Grew's information was forwarded to Admiral Kimmel in Hawaii with an evaluation by Naval Intelligence stating that "based on known data regarding the present disposition and deployment of Japanese naval and army forces no move against Pearl Harbor appears imminent or planned for the foreseeable future."

That seemed to invalidate Ambassador Grew's report, and Admiral Kimmel promptly dismissed it. Unfortunately, in the typical fashion of intelligence bureaucracies, no one ever ventured very far out on the limb. The operative phrases—"the *present* disposition and deployment" and "for the *foreseeable* future"—were not italicized or otherwise stressed in the evaluation provided to Admiral Kimmel. Since the report from Tokyo was placed in the category of unsubstantiated rumors, both Admiral Kimmel, in dismissing it, and ONI, in emphasizing the qualifying words, could claim to be in the right.

The fascination with high-level diplomacy continued to hold OP-20-GZ as well as the privileged inner circle at the summit of the U.S. government in its grip. Admiral Nomura had been sent as ambassador to Washington early in 1941, and "preliminary conversations" aimed at resolving U.S.-Japanese disagreements began in the spring in both Washington and Tokyo, although the talks made little progress. PURPLE, however, enabled the Americans in Washington to eavesdrop on the dialogue between Ambassador Nomura and the Japanese minister of foreign affairs in order to learn their real attitudes and goals.

But the U.S.-Japanese talks were upstaged by reports from Europe in Magic emanating as usual from the PURPLE machine. By April 1941 Japanese Ambassador Oshima in Berlin was informing his government that a German surprise attack on the Soviet Union was imminent. Commander Kramer wrote a GZ Memorandum summarizing all the information from Magic, most of it sent by Oshima, directly bearing on German plans for attacking the Soviet Union. Through no fault of Kramer's, the material he prepared very nearly betrayed the secret that we had broken the PURPLE machine cipher.

Undersecretary of State Sumner Welles, one of the recipients of the material from Kramer, took it upon himself without authorization from his superiors to show the original documents to Soviet Ambassador Constantine Oumansky. Welles hoped in this way to impress upon Soviet leaders the seriousness of the situation and give them a timely warning against the impending German aggression. It might, he thought, even lead to a rupture of relations between the USSR and Nazi Germany which would be advantageous to the West.

As often happened in such cases, Welles had misunderstood the situation. Oumansky, a clever man as well as an opportunist, knew that Stalin had ignored similar warnings from other sources. One such source was Richard Sorge, a Communist and GRU (Soviet Military Intelligence) agent operating under the cover of a German correspondent in Japan, who had done invaluable work as a spy, not only ferreting out Japanese top-secret information but penetrating the German embassy and becoming a crony of the ambassador. Ultimately, like Kramer, he would predict the exact date, June 22, of Hitler's attack on the Soviet Union. Other Soviet agents produced similar information, but Stalin would not even pay heed to his own agents. So Oumansky (who was later killed in a mysterious airplane crash in Mexico) knew better than to risk Stalin's wrath by reporting Welles's information in the form of a warning to Moscow.

Instead Oumansky found a better use for the information. He reported to Moscow the obvious *source* of the material shown to him by Welles. Probably acting on instructions from Moscow, he tried to curry favor with the Germans by alerting Dr. Hans Thomsen, the German chargé d'affaires in Washington, to the fact that the United States was reading Oshima's enciphered messages to Tokyo. Thomsen informed Berlin, and the German government promptly passed on a warning to Oshima.

In all likelihood this was not the only time Soviet officials learned about American code breaking. During World War II Soviet Intelligence exploited the opposition to the Chiang Kai-shek regime in American left-wing circles by penetrating organizations formed to work against Chiang Kai-shek and obtaining secret information from them. Some sympathizers inside the U.S. government fed classified documents to a magazine called *Amerasia* for ostensible use in articles criticizing the Kuomintang and praising the Chinese Communists. These sympathizers were concentrated in the Far Eastern desk of the State Department and the same section of ONI. In June 1945 the FBI arrested a number of persons in connection with the case; among documents seized in the *Amerasia* office in New York was a long report describing how the United States had broken Japanese codes. It would have been surprising, given the pro-Soviet leanings of some members of the group, if copies of the documents had not been secretly forwarded to Moscow.

The warning given to Oshima should have been enough to make the Japanese discontinue use of the PURPLE machine and introduce a newer, and presumably more secure, cryptographic system. Much to the astonishment of the Americans, who were fully aware of the crisis from intercepted messages, the Japanese conducted an investigation that ended with the verdict that the information from Berlin was incorrect and that, while other systems might have been compromised, the Type No. 97 (PURPLE) cipher machine had not been compromised.

The reason was that Japan's leading cryptographers could not accept the possibility that the Type No. 97 cipher machine had been broken. They were convinced beyond all doubt that the machine was invulnerable to attacks by enemy cryptanalysts. Even after the war they persisted in the same belief, remaining convinced that the United States could not have broken their Type No. 97 machine by cryptanalysis alone and that the machine had somehow been stolen from one of Japan's overseas installations.

Commander Kramer's GZ Memorandum, correctly predicting

the German attack on the Soviet Union, only increased top-level interest in PURPLE. After the Japanese moved into Indochina in July 1941 and the United States retaliated with an oil embargo that threatened to leave Japan without sufficient fuel for its military machine once reserves had been used up, the deterioration of the situation was matched by a quickening of the tempo of the negotiations. The Japanese side felt a real sense of urgency and recognized that the only alternative to an early settlement was war. Still preoccupied with the war in Europe, President Roosevelt, however, left the task of negotiating with the Japanese to Secretary of State Hull. Thus Roosevelt showed his indifference to the negotiations with Japan, for he customarily bypassed Hull in diplomatic matters he perceived to be important. In consequence, some of the key decisions that doomed a successful outcome of the negotiations—if indeed there had ever been any possibility of success—were actually made by Hull without consulting the president.

The pace of negotiations grew still more hectic after Ambassador Kurusu was dispatched by Premier Hideki Tojo to Washington in order to "assist" Admiral Nomura in bringing the negotiations to a conclusion. Kurusu's real task was to keep the Americans in the dark as to Japan's real intentions, for opinion in Tokyo had hardened to the point where Japanese leaders reached agreement on the date for the beginning of hostilities unless the United States had come to terms before then.

The Magic obtained from PURPLE during this period was as much a part of the deception as the Japanese diplomatic effort itself. Since even the Ministry of Foreign Affairs was kept in ignorance about Japan's plans for a surprise attack, there was little beyond the framework of the negotiations that could be learned from communications with Tokyo's emissaries in Washington.

Nevertheless, OP-20-G and SIS worked diligently in tandem to read and translate the enciphered diplomatic traffic in PURPLE during this period. Meanwhile OP-20-GZ allowed other intercepted messages to pile up in incoming baskets. This applied, for example, to messages from the Japanese consulate in Honolulu, which actually originated from an agent of Japanese Naval Intelligence operating under diplomatic cover. This agent was reporting, at Tokyo's request, intelligence concerning U.S. warships in Pearl Harbor—the movements of those ships in and out of the harbor as well as their exact anchorages.

Although Japanese consulates elsewhere were also providing detailed intelligence, it might have been thought that Honolulu merited special attention in view of the fact that the U.S. Pacific Fleet was based at Pearl Harbor. But ONI considered the reports from Honolulu to be no more than low-level intelligence, and this rather scornful appraisal found its reflection in the low priority assigned to the intercepts by OP-20-GZ.

In late November—at a time when Yamamoto's Pearl Harbor task force had already sortied from Tankan Bay (Hitokappu Wan) in the remote Kuriles and was at sea, bound for Hawaii—OP-20-GZ was busy handling an assortment of messages that pointed to the acuteness of the crisis without providing any more definite information. Tokyo set up an open code to be used in weather broadcasts over the radio to alert Japanese installations abroad that war was imminent with the United States, Great Britain, or the Soviet Union, as the case might be. Other intercepted messages conveyed instructions for the burning of confidential documents and destruction of codes and ciphers.

No one with access to these decrypted messages could fail to see that Japan was on the verge of initiating hostilities in a new area. The American strategists, however, remained confident that Japan would never be reckless or foolish enough to launch a *direct* attack that would force the United States to go to war. For them the only question was whether the Japanese would move south into Thailand, Malaya, and the Dutch East Indies or north against Siberia and the Soviet Far East.

The Japanese meanwhile had made their preparations for the Pearl Harbor attack without having to resort to their normal communications. At the same time they introduced new call signs but continued to use some of the old ones and kept up an apparently normal volume of messages in home waters which indicated to American specialists in traffic analysis that the Imperial Navy's carriers remained as before in the Inland Sea. Without contrary information, U.S. communications intelligence officers would only report a negative finding to the higher command: there was nothing to indicate an immediate Japanese threat. In the absence of other information OP-20-GZ had only Magic as an intelligence source. Even though the amount of information of military value in Magic had increased, there was an inclination in OP-20-GZ at that time to consider such information of slight importance.

At a much later date Phil Cate opened one of the IBM runs and showed me the message *"Niitakasan wo nobore,"* which Admiral Yamamoto had sent to the carrier task force bound for Hawaii as a signal that the attack was definitely to proceed as planned.

"What would you have done if you had been able to read this message at the time?" I asked Cate.

"Nothing," he said with a puckish glance. "It wouldn't have meant anything to us."

"Wouldn't you have assumed it had some special meaning?"

"Probably."

"But it wouldn't have pointed to Pearl Harbor."

"No. Maybe something big—even war. But more than that——" Cate shrugged.

On Saturday, December 6, 1941, the people of GZ were scheduled to work only a half day. Most of them were looking forward to the weekend, which held the promise of unusually balmy weather for that time of year. Only Dorothy Edgers, a new addition to the staff, was looking eagerly for something to do before she went home.

From the In-box she picked out a lengthy intercept that happened to be one of the Japanese Naval Intelligence officer's messages from Honolulu, sent three days earlier. The more she read, the more excited she became, and her conviction grew that the intercept was of unusual importance.

Later Dorothy recalled: "It was about a set of signals to be used in sending information about the U.S. fleet in port. There were to be lights in the windows of certain houses or bonfires on certain peaks visible from the seaward side. There was also something about radio advertisements."

Dorothy found this message so interesting that she put everything else aside to work on it. Then she showed it to her brother, Fred Woodruff.

"What do you think?" she asked.

Fred nodded. He was not one to display much of what he really thought. "Show it to Al Kramer."

She continued working on the message even after she was due to go home for the day. When Kramer finally appeared later in the afternoon, she spoke to him about the message. By her account, Kramer scanned the text very rapidly, just standing there. He handed it back to her without a word.

"What should I do with it?" Dorothy asked.

"It can wait until Monday."

Dorothy was not aware that Kramer had already immersed himself in the first parts of the fourteen-part message that was coming in over the PURPLE machine. He had seen enough to know that the message contained a diplomatic note that was obviously Japan's answer to the United States in the ongoing negotiations. The note itself had been written or translated into English and therefore required no translation by the Japanese embassy in Washington or, for that matter, by the translators of GZ.

Yet if he had not been so preoccupied with the fourteen-part message in PURPLE, Kramer would have certainly realized that the signal system described in Dorothy Edgers's message was a *visual* one meant to be observed by Japanese submarines standing offshore at Oahu while the radio ads could be picked up by the submarines or even surface ships not far away from Hawaii. As a matter of fact, on December 6, the day before the Pearl Harbor attack, the radios of the Japanese task force were tuned in on Honolulu stations that came in loud and clear.

It looked like another relaxing weekend in Washington, but

CLIMB THE HIGHEST MOUNTAIN

after almost everyone had gone home on Saturday afternoon the traffic in PURPLE suddenly became exceedingly busy. First of all came a pilot message alerting the Japanese embassy to the fourteen-part message with the text of a diplomatic note that Ambassadors Nomura and Kurusu were to deliver personally to Secretary of State Hull. The pilot message did not specify, however, exactly when these emissaries should deliver the note. The Ministry of Foreign Affairs also deliberately delayed transmission of the vital fourteenth part until the last possible moment. It was the fourteenth part that contained not only the vital concluding passages of the note but the time set for delivery, December 7, at 1:00 P.M. Washington time.

Because of some technical difficulties the first thirteen parts did not get into Kramer's hands until 9:00 P.M. on Saturday night. But the crucial fourteenth part, the really significant part of the whole communication, did not reach him until Sunday morning. That Saturday night Kramer, always a disciplined and conscientious officer, make it his task to drive around Washington in order to deliver the available text to the president and other top officials. Although this text was sufficient to anticipate a rupture of negotiations, there was nothing that definitely indicated war or an imminent attack.

Even when the crucial fourteenth part of the message was delivered late Sunday morning to all the key officials including Gen. George Marshall and Admiral Stark, no one seemed to consider it necessary to take any action, except for a last-minute message to General Short and Admiral Kimmel in Hawaii, advising them to be on the alert.

Thinking it unwise to use the telephone, General Marshall ordered that this message be sent by the fastest safe means. Left to subordinates, it resulted in the message going via Western Union to San Francisco and via RCA radio from there to Honolulu. A messenger on a bicycle was delivering the message to Pearl Harbor just as the bombs started to rain down.

The final words of the Japanese note struck some as an ultimatum but seemed to arouse little urgency among these leaders: "The

Japanese government regrets to have to notify hereby the American government that in view of the attitude of the American government it cannot but consider that it is impossible to reach an agreement through further negotiations."

The timing of delivery of the note at 1:00 P.M. on December 7 had been chosen to coincide with the dawn attack on Pearl Harbor, allowing for the difference in time zones. Due to the Japanese embassy's difficulties in retyping the note, however, Ambassadors Nomura and Kurusu had to request a delay in meeting with Hull and delivered the note only after the attack had already taken place.

The Pearl Harbor defeat and especially the failure to foresee the attack acutely affected everyone in OP-20-GZ, and months later, when I reported for duty, a pall of gloom still hung over the branch. There was also a cloud over its former chief, Commander Kramer, who would be called on to testify before navy boards of inquiry and in congressional investigations over a period of years, even when the war was over. But Rosey Mason had replaced Kramer and, with the introduction of new people into the branch, was injecting an equally new and aggressive spirit into its work.

By the time of my arrival GZ's work focused on the war, and for many months we scarcely paid attention to diplomatic traffic. Only occasionally would there be a message from Berlin in which Ambassador Oshima, who had strong German sympathies and enjoyed the confidence of Nazi leaders, passed on some political or military information of value, or a dispatch from another capital like Moscow that fanned our interest for a brief interval.

I had moved out of the room I temporarily shared with Jack Hall before his marriage to Robin, and now I was forced to look around again for a place to live. I moved into a house where Walter Nichols, another classmate from Harvard, had rented a room. It was a rather attractive residence on a quiet street in Chevy Chase, within walking distance of Connecticut Avenue, where I caught my bus. There was a garden hemmed in by tall hedges with beds of roses and other flowers, particularly, in those spring days, the lilac bushes that offered splashes of white and purple and exuded a heady scent.

The drawback of my new home turned out to be our landlady, an Englishwoman of fifty or so with dyed red hair, false teeth, and a lumpy figure, who seemed to have an excessive interest in young men. In this she faced competition from a young daughter who could have inspired the nymphette Lolita of Nabokov's novel. The landlady was a widow and rented out most of the rooms in the house to augment a pension left by her late husband, a civil servant.

Other tenants included a young unmarried couple, government employees, who had set up housekeeping in the basement. They threw big parties every Saturday night which nearly always ended in a brawl caused by the jealousy of the host or hostess.

Tiring of this merry-go-round, I began searching for a new place to live. Luck was with me because around this time Sy Millstein arrived in Washington and invited me to move in with him. He had succeeded in renting a master bedroom with private bath on the second floor of a private house owned by a Ukrainian family named Gindlin. Soon Sy and I expanded our mutual interests by becoming partners in the ownership of a car, a 1937 Oldsmobile, and he started teaching me how to drive.

We also began to lead an active social life that revolved around girls, with occasional double dating. In this period a daughter of the Gindlin family introduced me to one of her girl friends, a slender brunette, very pretty, shy, with a sweet, serious face. A native of Montana, she worked for the National Research Council, on Constitution Avenue, within walking distance of the Navy Department. Her name was Charlotte Whelan. In a short time we were seeing each other with increasing frequency and I made the acquaintance of her family, except for a brother who was assigned to a gun crew on a munitions ship in the Pacific.

Despite the driving lessons, I continued to take the bus down to the Navy Department on Constitution Avenue. Every morning I walked over one block to Connecticut Avenue from Fessenden

6. The Navy Department Building in Washington, D.C., where OP-20-G was headquartered during the first eight months of war with Japan. *National Archives.*

Street where we lived. There I caught an express bus that took me directly to Constitution Avenue and let me out in front of the Navy Building. In the evening I could get another express bus in front of the building and ride back out Connecticut Avenue.

Ralph Cory was preparing for his departure, and one night he invited me to dinner at his house in Maryland. We drove up a long lane under graceful elms in gathering twilight, stopping in front of a modest bungalow some distance removed from its neighbors. It was a strangely somber evening. I met his wife and we had some drinks before dinner, but no one had much to say.

As conversation lagged, I looked around at the interior of the house, which had been furnished with typical department store furniture and seemed to lack a personal touch, except for family photographs placed at random here and there, on a mantelpiece, on top of an upright piano, on several tables. We sat down to dinner in a gloomily lit dining room. Cory pulled himself together and talked a little about sailing on Chesapeake Bay. He lapsed into silence, and when I asked him about his experiences in Japan he replied with only a few words. His wife served the meal and sat across from him, looking at him intently from time to time and only occasionally acknowledging my presence with some query about the food or other trivial remark. So we sat through dinner and then moved back to the living room for coffee. As soon as a decent interval had passed, I thanked them for their hospitality and took my leave.

Cory left OP-20-GZ not long afterward to enter the Marine Corps as a second lieutenant. I never saw him again. Nevertheless, I was to have news of him later under tragic circumstances.

CHAPTER 4

Visions Before Midnight

EVERY morning it was my practice to read the *Washington Post* during my bus ride down Connecticut Avenue toward the Navy Building, and the news of the war continued to be gloomy.

The German siege of Leningrad had not been broken during the winter, and although Hitler's drive on Moscow had been blunted the previous autumn, the Nazi armies were certain to renew the offensive as soon as the spring mud hardened. In North Africa British forces based at Tobruk could expect to face an all-out assault by Rommel. And in the Pacific, like a patient all too aware of his weakness after a near-fatal illness, we tried to recuperate but waited for the next blow to fall, wondering how to cope with the Japanese, who seemed invincible after a long chain of victories.

But I had little time for long thoughts about the unfavorable war situation. I began to get deeper into the work of GZ. Communications intelligence concerning the Imperial Navy's plans and operations were a focus of attention for Rosey Mason himself, and other old hands like Lt. Pres Currier, who, I was told, had risen from the enlisted ranks because of his cryptanalytical talents, and civilians like Fred Woodruff, Phil Cate, and Dorothy Edgers.

Another officer of superlative ability who joined Mason in the same work about this time was Comdr. Rufus Taylor, a dark, intense man of medium height and build, obviously destined to have a brilliant career. He lacked Mason's abrasive personality—a possible plus factor for him. Indeed, Taylor possessed leadership qualities that were hardly second to Mason's, but he was also pleasant and attractive in manner, a person who seemed likely to enhance any social occasion.

There was of course a certain distance between junior naval officers like myself and the more senior types like Mason and Taylor, as in any military organization. Nevertheless, rank distinctions in GZ were in many ways less important than they would have been at sea. The work took precedence over everything else, and those who could contribute to it received respect in accordance with their contribution rather than their rank.

The people of GZ afforded interesting contrasts. They were all in some way linked to Japan—by birth, or circumstances, or career—but outside their present work they had almost nothing in common.

The regular naval officers, Annapolis graduates, had been assigned to Japanese language studies in the expectation that the Imperial Navy might become a major adversary of the U.S. Navy. Like the young Foreign Service officers, the Kennans and Bohlens, who were trained as Soviet specialists against the time when the United States would recognize the Soviet Union, these naval officers went into training for a possible war with Japan, but unlike the diplomats, who were forced by the absence of official relations with the USSR to study the Russian language in Riga, Latvia, then on the periphery of the USSR, the naval officers could pursue their study of Japanese in the potential enemy's capital, Tokyo.

From the beginning, however, the Japanese assignment represented for most of the officers simply one facet of their naval career, which remained at the center of their lives. There were a few who did not possess the same degree of dedication. A lesser member of the elite group of language officers discussed his life in other terms: "Annapolis?" he said, his mouth twisting as if he were tasting something very bitter. "It was like a four-year prison sentence." He planned to resign from the navy as soon as the war was over. But the others went about their work like professional boxers preparing for a bout; they had learned their opponent's secrets and now intended to demolish him in the ring. Then they would go on to future bouts against other opponents.

I associated myself with the next group made up, essentially, of academically oriented civilians. Nicer than most of them, Bob Paine had no academic pretensions but could have been a stand-in for all the professors who came to Washington then and later, professors belonging to almost every discipline, Oriental languages, English, French and German literature, linguistics, statistics, mathematics, physics, and astronomy—indeed the faculty of a fine university could have been set up on the spot. Those assigned to GZ had been drawn intellectually and aesthetically toward the Japanese language, culture, and history; many had spent years off and on in Japan, which had also become involved in their personal lives through the accident of birth or by marriage. The group included businessmen or missionaries whose first interest ran along other lines but who had been propelled by circumstances into a similar encounter with Japan.

Finally, there was a group of civilians bound by ties of blood to Japan. They had lived virtually as Japanese among the Japanese, and they were torn by an ambivalence, a riptide of love and hostility, that surged with irresistible force out of their pasts. Racial prejudices also existed in Japan, and the Japanese looked down, for example, on the Ainu, an ancient and primitive tribe that resembled our American Indians in being the earliest inhabitants of the country. The Japanese looked down, too, on the Eta, the untouchables of Japan, just as they did on the Koreans and other Asians in their midst. They disliked the white race and despised still more those who had an admixture of Japanese blood. People like Cate and Woodruff, who belonged to this group, found themselves in a purgatory that seemed to bring out some less admirable traits—in Woodruff's case, a strong strain of arrogance.

I talked to Woodruff about his work. "It's just routine," he said gruffly.

"Aren't you worried about the responsibility?"

"What responsibility?"

"Well, I mean, if you miss anything—if you make a mistake——"

He shrugged and gave me a pale smile. "I don't make mistakes."

I observed the way things were done. If the message seemed to be important, Mason would handle it himself or assign other cryptanalysts to the task of working over unrecovered code groups, dropping whatever else they had been involved in. Adopting these methods, they became adept in decoding Japanese fleet communications, and there were virtually no secrets that could be kept from us. Mason assigned me to work with Bob Paine on tactical communications, which included contact reports, such as attacks and sightings.

Japan's military successes in the first part of the war had also created problems. The area of conquest had brought Japanese forces as far south as Singapore along the continent of Asia and to far-flung islands in the Pacific: the Philippines, the East Indies, New Guinea, the Bismarcks, the Gilberts, as well as American possessions like Guam and Wake. Later it would take them into the western Aleutians in the far north and the Solomons well to the south, threatening to outflank Australia. The Imperial Navy's resources were strained to maintain installations in these numerous distant locations, to operate warships in such widely separate areas, and to carry out all the complex and burdensome supply operations.

The difficulties of the Imperial Navy opened up opportunities for us in communications intelligence. First of all, it was by no means a simple task to distribute code books and other secret communications materials to all the units and installations, separated by thousands of miles of ocean, that required them. When a code was due to be changed, those responsible for communications security had to ensure that the new book was already in the possession of all proper users before the new code could go into effect.

If the new code book had not been distributed to all the normal recipients, the danger existed that some unit that had not received the new one would request a repetition of a message in the old code; in the event that the original sender took a message that had already been transmitted in the new code and repeated it in the old one as requested, the new code would be partly compromised.

Later the Japanese tried to get around this problem of distribution by dividing the total area needing coverage into a number of zones, in each of which a new code book could be introduced apart from the other zones. This scheme, however, enjoyed limited success. According to the basic idea, the new code book might already be in use in one zone while the old code book continued to be used in another zone, without running the risk of compromising the new system. In practice it did not work so well because the zones could not always be separated so neatly.

Another negative effect of the distribution problem was the danger of a code remaining in effect too long simply because of the delay in distributing the new code book. The more time the enemy cryptanalysts had to break a code and the more messages they had available for study, the more likelihood there was that the code would be read.

In addition, the wide dissemination of secret communications materials, unavoidable in the circumstances, was accompanied by increased risk for the Imperial Navy. As long as the Japanese were on the offensive and continued to hold the initiative, the risk was minimal. But once the enemy could go over to the attack, no one could predict with certainty where he might strike, and the possibility existed that those materials might fall into the enemy's hands, thereby compromising one or another code.

Taking into account all such factors, the Imperial Navy had ample cause to worry about the security of its communications.

Nevertheless, there were other problems that possibly received less attention from the Japanese. One of the more important of those problems happened to be an attitude, a state of mind, that governed their approach to communications security.

The Japanese attitude toward communications security was affected by a conviction that foreigners, especially Westerners, could not really master their language. Consequently, they believed that the language itself offered sufficient protection. A true story, which Ki Cammann told me, illustrated the Oriental point of view: A friend of his from New York's American Museum of Natural History, who had been born in China and spoke several dialects fluently, found himself in a remote area of China while on an archaeological expedition. The American, who had temporarily lost his bearings, encountered an old man with some children and asked him in Chinese for directions, but the old man simply shook his head. Finally the American gave up, but as he walked away he heard the old man say to the children, in the very same speech, "If I didn't know he was a foreigner, I'd swear that man spoke to me in our language."

Of course we made the most of our opportunities for reading the Japanese codes. At that stage of the war, with the preponderance of strength clearly on their side, we desperately needed all the help we could get.

Bob Paine, dressed in tweeds which bestowed upon him the look of a kindly Oxford don, sat next to me and flung open the IBM runs to explain the contents. The details were clear even though my thoughts wandered. The code breaker (something in Paine's careful New England accent told me) was like a poet in that he started with a blank page. With all the soul-searching and groping, the poet sought the answer within himself while the code breaker looked elsewhere, into some other person's consciousness . . . Still, I told myself with a secret smile, what did a code breaker and a poet really have in common? Imagination perhaps. The people in traffic analysis could be of enormous help by telling us whether a message had originated with a man-of-war or merchant vessel or shore-based headquarters, but even then the message remained elusive without the precious gift of imagination, sometimes stimulated by a word here and there. Yet what poet had not responded at times to the thrill of a certain word?

And as Bob Paine went on and on, pointing out things to me in the same kindly professorial tone, none of which, surprisingly, I missed, I could reflect that the juxtaposition of code breaker and poet was not entirely a product of my imagination. Indeed a few literary detectives had tried to turn Shakespeare, the greatest poet of all, into a cryptographer—more precisely, Shakespeare as Francis Bacon's alter ego. Using methods disdained by any competent cryptanalyst, they proved to their own satisfaction that Bacon, supposedly reluctant to risk damage to his reputation as a statesman, had allowed a semiliterate Shakespeare to pose as the playwright while embedding his own enciphered claim to authorship in the texts of the plays. Bacon, in his voluminous writings, had treated the subject of cryptography, and therefore proponents of this odd theory could find a Freudian admission in the words, "He that plots to be the only figure among ciphers, is the decay of the whole age."

Leaving such misleading questions aside, I leaned to the view that there was a stronger analogy with music. Like the musician, the cryptanalyst dealt with symbols and had to look beyond them, to the music that lay behind; although time was important for the musician, rhythm had a special meaning for the code breaker or cryptanalyst, a rhythm that he could identify and correlate and from which, eventually, he could extract a particular sense. The cryptanalyst's rhythm was the rhythm of symbols, but underlying it was the rhythm of language which unavoidably, at any number of removes, became the hard bedrock of codes. Therefore the cryptanalyst looked for the cadence of symbols, always hoping to discover the cadence of language.

Nonetheless, language was not the same for everybody. The

American wrote after his own fashion, and that was rooted in the national psychology. So did the Japanese. No code breaker could hope to penetrate the mystery of a code or cipher without regard for *the* language, culture, or psychology—the whole fabric of that people's soul. It would not do simply to count up the frequency of letters in an alphabet as in Edgar Allan Poe's famous tale "The Gold Bug," except on the most elementary level.

Despite my present collaboration with Bob Paine, I had the impression that the cryptanalyst's mind was one that had to function in isolation. While there were undoubtedly moments when cryptanalysts needed to exchange ideas, each one generally was obliged to follow his own lonely path, not unlike creative artists who seldom functioned well as collaborators. It was not like the intricate passages through a maze which could be penetrated in only one way; for each mind the light went on at a different point in response to different stimuli and illuminated the goal from a different direction. The word I wanted to apply was *inspiration,* which, in my view, would always be greater than the aggregate of all the information in the brain where it originated.

As we studied the material before us, Mason came over and stood nearby, looking down at the runs we were examining. Small beads of perspiration covered his balding head, and his face was more flushed than usual. But he did not speak. He merely grunted and moved away again.

"What was that all about?" I said in a low voice to Bob.

Bob tossed his pencil down on the desk. "He wants us to know that he's keeping an eye on us. No loafing. No trivial conversation."

"Oh."

"Well," Bob said with a glance at his watch, "it's time to refresh ourselves. Care for a spot of lunch?"

We sat in the cafeteria on one of the upper decks of the Navy Building with silverware and crockery clattering around us and an incessant rumble of voices. Many khaki and some blue uniforms, a sprinkling of civilian clothing. I picked at the chef's salad bowl I had chosen for lunch, spearing a piece of ham or a crisp wedge of lettuce.

"Do you like the salad?" Bob asked, smiling.

"Not much."

"It looks like a mixture of leaves and grass."

"That's how it tastes."

Bob made a face. "The stew doesn't amount to much either."

We were silent for a while, both making a half-hearted attempt to eat. Finally I broke the silence. "Why did you come to Washington, Bob?"

"Now that you ask," he said doubtfully, "I don't really know."

I waited, and he went on: "You could say I wanted to help my country. I thought that my knowledge of Japanese might be of some use."

"Obviously it is. But why did you choose to remain a civilian? They would have given you a commission if you'd wanted it."

Bob grinned. "Can you picture me in uniform? Besides, everyone in my family preferred it that way—my wife, my children. I wanted to have the freedom not only to come but also to go."

"I understand. Still, this is a far cry from being a curator at the Boston Museum of Fine Arts. Studying Japanese prints and that sort of thing."

I stopped suddenly and began to smile.

"What's so amusing?" Bob asked.

"I was just imagining what it will be like when some of your old friends from Harvard come down here. What will the military make of them?"

"What will they make of the military?" Bob said promptly.

"Unfortunately the military have the upper hand right now. How long do you think you'll stay on?"

"Only as long as they really need me."

"Then you'll return home to Cambridge?"

"For the rest of my life," Bob said. He made it sound like a prayer. "What will you do after the war, Ed?"

"I don't know. I can't even see an end to the war."

"What kind of a career were you planning before the war?"

"Different things. At one time I wanted to teach languages— but I think what I really wanted was to travel. Then I had the idea of becoming a journalist. Now I think I might like to write."

"Writing is fine if you have a private income," Bob put in. "There's not much money in writing. Unless you write best-sellers."

"That's what I'm going to do—write best-sellers."

"The only successful writer I've met is J. P. Marquand." A wry look came over Bob's face. "I don't like the fellow. I was at a dinner party with him once, and I couldn't have felt more uncomfortable. I had the feeling he was just making mental notes for one of his blasted books."

"Wasn't he rather hard on proper Bostonians?"

"Let's say he didn't make himself popular in my circles," Bob said, standing up. "Well, we'd better get back if we don't want to make Mason mad."

We worked together steadily all afternoon. Late in the day Mason came back again and looked over our shoulders. We both looked up. He grunted. "How're you coming along?"

"Good, sir," I said enthusiastically.

"Don't let up," he said crisply. "Get on with the work. I want results."

"Aye, aye, sir."

Bob Paine had been looking more and more distressed. Now he suddenly spoke up: "Commander, we only *started* working together this morning."

"Then get on with it. This is no tea party, goddamnit!" Mason snapped and, turning on his heel, walked away.

Bob's angry glance followed him. "I'm glad he didn't say *Boston* tea party," Bob said under his breath.

We reacted with more amusement to the efforts of Lieutenant Brotherhood, our immediate superior, to put pressure on us. From time to time he came breezing by, then circled back to ask, in a cheerful voice, "How's it going?"

Brotherhood, a former insurance or real estate man—no one seemed to be sure which—had almost no knowledge of Japanese, and his efforts to pretend to some knowledge made him appear foolish to my colleagues. He was a tall, dark, crinkly-haired man, of slender build, whose affable manner reflected the sales pitch of his civilian occupation.

Brotherhood had a peculiar habit that soon caught my attention. Whenever I approached his desk, he seemed to be looking down at something in the open center drawer. Suddenly noticing my approach, he would slam the desk drawer shut and turn the key in the lock.

"What on earth is he up to?" I asked Paine one day.

"I haven't the foggiest notion," Bob said automatically, then abruptly contradicted himself. "Yes, I do. He's reading the GZ Daily Summary and doesn't want any of us to see it."

The GZ Daily Summary contained our translations of the messages we had worked on but naturally gave a complete overview of the work done in GZ on a given day. Nevertheless, some of the others felt offended that they should have been deprived of knowledge to which Brotherhood had ready access.

Meanwhile Sy Millstein, my roommate, was teaching me to drive a car, and I started having nightmares that became a strange amalgam of crises at the wheel and abortive attempts at code breaking. In one nightmare, which was repeated several times, I found myself desperately trying to control the wheel of the car with one hand while I sought, full of panic, to use a code book with the other hand in order to learn my destination.

During the day the problems appeared less bizarre. The actual work in breaking a code reminded me of a pack of hounds in pursuit of hares that had fled across the countryside in different directions. You followed a scent until you came to a cross-scent that looked more promising, and followed that scent to another cross-scent that looked still more productive, until perhaps you wound up in an impassable thicket and were forced to backtrack to one of the scents you had abandoned earlier.

Depending on one's inclination or state of mind, one could follow a particular scent to its logical conclusion, or else pursue a cross-scent that passed over a number of other scents until it too was lost.

But the analogy of hounds baying after hares (the unrecovered code groups) also had its limitations, for it begged the question of form. Apart from the form of a code as a whole, the content found a reflection in archetypes that possessed specific forms of their own. For example, in cryptanalytic communications of a tactical nature, the usual format of a message reporting a submarine attack ran along the following lines:

"At _____ hours we were attacked by an enemy submarine with _____ torpedoes. We suffered _____ hit(s) aft (forward) (amidships). Listing _____ degrees to port (starboard). We are losing way (dead in the water) (sinking). Our position: _____ North, _____ East."

This archetype would be reproduced in many messages with minor alteration. If, for example, the originator was reporting an attack on another ship in the convoy, the ship's name, _____ _____ *Maru* (the suffix given by the Japanese to all merchant ships), would appear at the beginning.

Another archetype was furnished by simple arrival or departure messages—sometimes a combination of both: "_____ _____ *Maru* departed RR (Japanese coordinates for Rabaul) on _____ (date) at _____ (hours) bound for RXE (Shortland). Estimated time of arrival _____ (date) _____ (hours)."

The essential element, therefore, was to identify an archetype which then offered all sorts of possibilities for the recovery of code groups with parallel meanings within a definite form. In addition, however, there was the possibility that certain code groups contained in one archetype could help in the identification of another archetype, as in the two examples of form already mentioned.

It made me recall my play as a child with an Erector set that provided pieces and strips of metal of various sizes and shapes, accompanied by nuts and bolts with which they could be joined at the whim of their owner. The child could realize his vision through construction, making the mind's vision take shape before his eyes.

The cryptanalyst's vision was conditioned by the archetype that he had come to see in his mind's eye. If the pieces of the Erector set represented code groups, he went about making a representation of the archetype, possibly in the shape of some cube. This cube could be connected by struts with another cube, a parallel construction. But the remaining pieces, triangular or round, had to be used differently; perhaps a tower was made to soar above the low profile of the initial structures. Depending on the available material, the cryptanalyst sought to realize his conception, and ideally, sooner or later, a beautiful, balanced architectural form would come into being.

All of life, I recognized (although why this surprised me I did not know), could be reduced into form and content, with one or the other sometimes preceding and sometimes following. Form could not exist without content, and content could not exist without form. As in life, so in codes: it was impossible to find one without the other. If you did not see the form, you could not find the content; if you failed to see the content, you would not recognize the form.

I watched; I studied; and I learned. I became aware that code breaking was not a *destructive* process but a cumulative process of *building* that came close to my evocation of the Erector set. But to make sure that the structure did not fall, there had to be constant testing of each recovered code group against its use in messages where the facts could be independently checked.

It seemed to me as if, without knowing it, I had been preparing all my life for this work. I had always been fond of higher mathematics as well as all sorts of problem solving. I enjoyed the most sophisticated riddles, crossword puzzles, and acrostics. I also liked the intricate calculations that went into chess. And in foreign language I had sought, in reality, to break a kind of code, to get at an inner meaning represented by symbols that were unknown to me in the beginning.

Now I realized that my mind and personality had a special affinity with code breaking, and aside from my recognition that reading our enemy's codes could make an important and probably even a key contribution to the war effort, I enjoyed the work for its own sake and felt an enormous intellectual stimulation (which made me feel a little guilty). In the course of time another truth became evident, instilling a certain humility: we were intimately involved in the life and death of human beings.

Although we had discussed the same subject previously, Bob Paine asked me again one day: "What are you going to do after the war?"

"Bob—I don't know. I wonder when the war will end. *If* it will end."

"You'll probably stay here," Bob said, displaying more insight than I possessed at the time.

"I have no idea. I can't even imagine what I'll do. At least you have a job to go back to."

"You'll stay," he repeated firmly.

Around the middle of April, even before I had arrived in Washington, GZ began to find hints that something big was in the air. It became clear that a massive buildup of forces was in progress at Rabaul in New Britain. Air and submarine reconnaissance soon confirmed the buildup, but its purpose was by no means clear. At this point we enjoyed some good fortune for a change. The scheduled change of a code was postponed, and as a result we were offered a golden opportunity to learn the precise nature of Japanese plans.

Rosey Mason drove his men hard, knowing that time was short: there had been a reprieve of one month in the change of the code. If anything was in the wind we had to find out about it now. People began to eat lunch at their desks, either bringing brown bags or fetching sandwiches from the kiosks whose unimaginative product was barely edible, and washing it down with soft drinks or coffee. No one needed to be told to go on working long after the rest of the building had emptied, and it was largely extreme weariness or importunate wives that broke the spell and drove people home.

Tension mounted in the sixth wing. Many people resented

Mason's bullying tactics, but only the civilians dared to show openly how much they resented his unrelenting pressure. Once Woodruff's hot temper flared. Quick, angry words quivered on the charged air and then dissipated. I heard my colleagues' mutterings—the kind, one could imagine, that precede ship mutinies— yet nothing out of the ordinary happened and the work went on.

It was a strange time because no one knew exactly what we were looking for. On the surface each person continued to work as before, combing the IBM runs for clues and conferring with similarly occupied colleagues when necessity arose.

Mason stayed in the forefront, leading the way. The lights burned late. Others could complain, but Mason won grudging respect by driving himself as hard as he drove others. Apart from the regular work, he gave out special assignments, selecting messages among current intercepts for their importance, sometimes, it seemed, on the sole basis of instinct. On occasion he personally assumed certain tasks; at other times he assigned one, two, even three people to work on a single message.

The playing of hare-and-hounds went on with one message after the other, a game repeated apparently interminably, but ultimately to good effect.

Gradually the evidence accumulated, little bits and pieces, parts of long messages, whole paragraphs, more rarely complete messages. Enough to reveal that the enemy was planning a seaborne invasion of Port Moresby to take place in early May. Port Moresby . . . The Japanese had already landed in northeastern New Guinea, but a towering mountain range blocked the way between the northern and southern coasts of the island, making any overland invasion a long and costly venture.

If a seaborne invasion succeeded, the Japanese would have a port directly opposite the northeastern tip of Australia, barely three hundred miles away, and the threat of a subsequent invasion would hang over that continent. Its defenses were so weak that in March 1942, on his arrival in Australia from besieged Corregidor, General MacArthur found only a single regular Australian division (all the others were fighting in the Middle East) and a mere twenty-five thousand U.S. troops. The situation had improved only marginally in the last month or six weeks.

In reality, however, the Japanese high command did not plan an immediate invasion of Australia. Their strategy at this point called for neutralizing air bases in northern Australia and moving down the chain of the Solomons and New Hebrides to invade Fiji, Samoa, and New Caledonia as a means of isolating Australia.

We knew that the Japanese planned to back up their invasion of Port Moresby with powerful naval forces. Although we still lacked many of the details, we had information indicating that the big punch would be delivered by a striking force that included the fleet carriers *Zuikaku* and *Shokaku*. Both carriers had participated in the attack on Pearl Harbor.

"Cincpac," the commander in chief of the Pacific Fleet, Adm. Chester Nimitz, immediately realized that the southern advance had to be met with the strongest forces we could muster on our side. Accordingly, he sent Adm. Frank Jack Fletcher's Task Force 17, built around the carriers *Lexington* and *Yorktown*, to the Solomon and Coral seas.

The postponement in the change of the code for one month had made it possible to ferret out information about the Port Moresby operation. Now the Japanese decided to postpone the change of code for still another month, a step that would affect the course of the whole war although it had no effect on the battle that was about to begin.

Bob Paine and I had to cope with a flood of messages as Japanese units reported on combat action. Unfortunately we were still at a stage that gave us little opportunity to extract valuable intelligence with which to help our own commanders. Japanese forces landing at Tulagi in the Solomons, in an attack timed to coincide with the invasion of Port Moresby, advised their headquarters on May 3 that they had been attacked by carrier-based planes (we heard later that the planes came from the *Yorktown*) inflicting, it appeared, slight damage. In the later phases of the Battle of the

Coral Sea, however, we remained in the dark, reading only scraps of the battle reports and learning about the course of the battle after it was all over.

The opposing carrier forces groping for each other attacked lesser foes at first. Fletcher's planes sank a small carrier, *Shoho*, that was supposed to provide air cover for the Japanese troop transports bound for Port Moresby, with the result that the transports turned back. Meanwhile the Japanese striking force located an oil tanker and a destroyer instead of Fletcher's Task Force 17 and sank both ships.

At last on May 8 each side fixed the location of the main adversary and launched all-out attacks involving a total of 240 carrier-based aircraft—a new style of naval battle in which the surface forces never sighted one another.

The two sides sustained damage, but the results seemed to be inconclusive. We looked upon the battle as an American victory because for the first time we held our own against the Imperial Navy. We shot down forty-three enemy planes while losing only thirty-three of our own. Both of the enemy fleet carriers, *Shokaku* and *Zuikaku*, had been temporarily put out of action, and one small carrier had been sunk. Against this we had to weigh the damage suffered by our two big carriers (until it became known that the *Lexington* had been lost after catching fire, at which point an American destroyer finally sank her with five torpedoes).

Coming as it did on the heels of the American surrender of the fortress of Corregidor in the Philippines, the Battle of the Coral Sea gave a much-needed boost to morale in both the United States and Australia. When all the details of the battle became available, it looked more and more as if we had actually suffered a defeat. The Imperial Navy had many carriers, the U.S. Navy had only a few, and in the battle we lost one of our precious remaining carriers. Yet later events proved that this pessimistic view was erroneous. It turned out that we had won an important strategic victory in the Battle of the Coral Sea. The seaborne invasion of Port Moresby had not only been repulsed but would never be attempted again. Moreover, the damage suffered by *Shokaku* as well as *Zuikaku*'s losses in flight personnel prevented those two carriers from taking part in the crucial Battle of Midway, whose outcome might have been altered by their participation.

Paine and I spent the next weeks studying the large pile of intercepts that had accumulated during the fighting in the Coral Sea. We compared the messages with battle reports provided by our own side. This enabled us to make significant inroads into the code, recovering many of the code groups we would soon need in the Battle of Midway. To some extent, by our work after the Coral Sea fighting we succeeded in confirming some of the reported results, particularly in losses sustained by the Japanese, and at the same time we had reason to hope that the next time around we would be in a much stronger position to provide valuable information when it was needed.

This time came sooner than we anticipated.

Even before the Battle of the Coral Sea reached its climax, Japan's Imperial General Headquarters issued an order of May 5 that we intercepted: "*CinC Combined Fleet will, in cooperation with the army, invade and occupy strategic points in the western Aleutians and Midway Island.*"

Although top-ranking Japanese military and naval leaders were more interested in pushing operations in the south, Admiral Yamamoto insisted that a major effort should be directed at the western Aleutians and Midway in order to lure Nimitz's Pacific Fleet into a decisive battle that would end in its destruction. Just as he had succeeded in winning agreement for a strike against Pearl Harbor over the objections of the Japanese high command, Yamamoto now succeeded in overriding similar objections in order to press the Midway operation. Neither Yamamoto nor his critics in Imperial General Headquarters had the slightest suspicion, however, that we would not be caught unawares as at Pearl Harbor but were fully informed about their plans for an attack on Midway.

Hundreds of messages originated from Yamamoto's headquarters aboard the superbattleship *Yamato* recalling some two hundred ships—carriers, battleships, cruisers, destroyers, mine-sweepers, tankers, and supply vessels—to take part in the huge and ambitious operation. GZ managed to read the majority of these messages. But, not content with what we had thus far, we engaged in an all-out effort to recover the 10 percent of other messages that still remained unread. We knew the main outlines of the opera-tion, but it was essential to learn as many details as possible in order to make certain that our commanders could plan to counter the enemy at vital points and bring about his defeat.

As usual, Mason himself determined which messages should be read, and he assigned members of his staff to recover the missing parts.

On May 20 Yamamoto spelled out those details in an opera-tions order that revealed all we needed to know. It became abun-dantly clear that the commander in chief of the Combined Fleet had assembled a gigantic force to ensure the success of the opera-tion: eleven battleships, five carriers, sixteen cruisers, and forty-nine destroyers.

Yamamoto's force was to sortie from the Inland Sea on May 27, the anniversary of Admiral Togo's decisive victory over the Russian fleet in Tsushima Strait, a battle in which Yamamoto himself had served as a young ensign.

Admiral Chuichi Nagumo commanded the Mobile Force of four big carriers escorted by two battleships, three cruisers, and eleven destroyers. His mission was to soften up Midway for the Occupation Force of troop transports approaching from the south-west to carry out an invasion of the island. Nagumo would lie in wait for the U.S. Pacific Fleet, which was expected to oppose the occupation of Midway. Meanwhile Admiral Yamamoto, preserving radio silence, planned to remain farther back with his superdread-nought *Yamato* and the other battleships. A diversionary force was to be detached for the invasion of the western Aleutians and bom-bardment of Dutch Harbor in the eastern Aleutians on June 3.

When the Pacific Fleet rushed south from the Aleutians or sortied from Pearl Harbor to protect Midway Island, Yamamoto's

7. Fleet Admiral Isoroku Yamamoto, Imperial Japanese Navy commander in chief, Japanese Combined Fleet.

submarine force would be lying in ambush, ready to inflict the initial damage. Then the numerically superior Japanese torpedo planes and dive bombers would deliver crushing blows, and after American air power had been eliminated, the battleships and heavy cruisers would move in for the kill. Result: complete destruction of the U.S. Pacific Fleet, opening up the way to Hawaii.

All that Nimitz could bring to bear to oppose this overwhelmingly powerful force were three fleet carriers, eight cruisers, and fourteen destroyers (most of the Pacific Fleet's battleships had been put out of action at Pearl Harbor). He also assigned nineteen submarines to cover the approaches to Midway. It seemed as if, even with forewarning, Nimitz faced a hopeless task.

Those May days were tense and frightening. Every day I made the same trip down Connecticut Avenue in the morning and back over the same route in the evening. Everything appeared so normal . . . and yet I could not help wondering about the shock waves that would engulf our world if Yamamoto's plan succeeded.

Washington in springtime had never been more beautiful. I looked at the peaceful traffic, the untroubled passersby—most of the men still in civilian clothes, pretty girls looking all the more seductive in their flimsy dresses without the coats they had worn all winter—and I asked myself what was going on in their minds. Did they have any inkling of what could happen? But there was nothing to disturb the outward appearance of peace. The fresh green grass, the flowering pink or white dogwood, the Japanese, newly rechristened "Korean," cherry trees in bloom around the Tidal Basin. At the noon hour I followed the drive under elms that curved around the Ellipse, emerging on the south side of the White House, clearly in view between the flower beds, and turned my steps toward F Street in the downtown area to mingle with the shoppers, all of whom seemed oblivious of the war.

"All this could change, perhaps overnight," I thought. "If the Pacific Fleet goes, there will be panic, especially on the West Coast."

My roommate, Sy Millstein, was unhappy. "I can't wait to get out of here," he told me. "D'you know what they've got me doing in ONI? Translating a Japanese dictionary of chemical terms, that's what."

"Where will you go?"

"Any place, Ed, just so it's not Washington. I've requested an assignment in the south Pacific."

8. Admiral Chuichi Nagumo, Imperial Japanese Navy, commander of the Mobile Force at the Battle of Midway.

It seemed to me that if we were beaten decisively at Midway there would be no place for us in the south Pacific. "Well, I wish you luck, Sy. Whatever happens," I added with a smile, "I can't picture you spending the rest of the war behind a desk."

Indeed, the situation was building to a climax in the central Pacific. Owing to his foreknowledge of Yamamoto's plans, Nimitz ordered the prompt recall of the carriers *Hornet* and *Enterprise* from the Coral Sea, where they had arrived too late to take part in that battle. He also recalled the crippled *Yorktown*, which underwent emergency repairs at Pearl Harbor and, almost miraculously, was ready to go to sea a few days after *Hornet* and *Enterprise*, to engage the Japanese striking force as it approached Midway. Moreover, Admiral King had diverted, on a temporary basis, several squadrons of heavy and medium bombers destined for MacArthur's southwest Pacific area, and Nimitz immediately sent the bombers to Midway.

The contribution of communications intelligence to the preparations for the Battle of Midway did not end there. Yamamoto had ordered his submarines to intercept the main body of the Pacific Fleet as it sortied from Pearl Harbor or rushed back from the Aleutians, but the Japanese submarines were not scheduled to be on station until June 1. Knowing this, Nimitz sent Adm. Raymond Spruance to sea with the U.S. carriers in advance of that date so that they were safely past the patrol line, *Hornet* and *Enterprise* on May 29, *Yorktown* on the thirty-first. This had an important bearing on the outcome of the battle, for instead of the Japanese it was the Americans who achieved surprise at Midway.

Paine and I had intensified our efforts before any new fighting erupted, profiting as much as possible from the traffic accumulated during the Battle of the Coral Sea. This had given us an interval of nearly a month which we exploited to the maximum, working feverishly in the knowledge that Midway loomed before us and we would be alone in providing information at that point.

The traffic with which we had to deal did not differ essentially from the usual run of codes. As a rule, codes make use of groups of numbers or letters, four or five depending on the code, arranged in an apparently random manner. Each of the numerical or alphabetical code groups has a value assigned to it in the code book: the group can stand for a whole sentence, phrase, word, letter, number, date, punctuation, message part number, or the like. Another type of group can represent a sentence or phrase containing one blank or dotted space to be filled in by the immediately following group. In Japanese or Chinese, both of which make use of ideographs, a code group representing a single character (or word) may combine with one or more of the following groups to form a compound word. Most code books are arranged in two parts: one part follows the format of a dictionary so that words or expressions can be looked up in their proper order, opposite the corresponding code group, while the other part follows the numerical or alphabetical order of the code groups, giving corresponding plain text values.

The messages that came to Paine and myself had been picked up by navy intercept stations and were forwarded through teletype channels to us in OP-20-G. The intercepted radio transmissions were in the form of single communications, with an originator and addressees, which, if already identified from the call signs by GX, had been filled in at the top. The code groups followed in vertical order on the sheets reproduced in OP-20-G, going down a column on the left side of the page; where we had already "recovered" a code group, that is, assigned it a plain text value, the text would be entered opposite the code group in the center of the page. Blanks remained in the message opposite code groups that had not yet been recovered. For the Japanese originator it had simply been a matter of breaking up the plain text and copying corresponding code groups out of the book in proper order. For the Japanese addressee the only task was to look up the code groups in the other part of the book and copy down the plain text values that made up the message. For us the task was a much larger one, and we had to do our utmost to find values for the missing code groups in our intercepts.

We knew that we had reached a climactic moment in the war. Without doubt, Paine and I were a part of that climactic moment, along with thousands of others much closer to the scene of action. Tolstoy denied that the Battle of Borodino was a turning point in Napoleon's invasion of Russia, maintaining that the end result would have been the same even if the battle had never been fought. But unlike Tolstoy we were certain that if there had been no Midway some other critical battle would have had to be fought in its stead.

On June 3 we saw a flurry of messages from Yamamoto's Aleutian carrier force attacking Dutch Harbor, mainly reporting ineffectual enemy air attacks. The results encouraged us to hope that we would be able to do an effective job as the battle developed, for we had little trouble in reading these coded messages. More messages were intercepted from the same force on the fourth, but by this time we found ourselves inundated with traffic from the Midway area, also reporting attacks by land-based planes which, like the ones in the Aleutians, had left the Japanese warships unscathed.

The atmosphere in GZ almost crackled with tension, laden with electricity like the atmosphere just before a thunderstorm. The large room was painted in the functional gray of the navy and filled with plain long wooden tables and open deep cabinets whose shelves held fat IBM runs and other reference or research materials.

Against one wall a large chart of the central and northern Pacific had been hung, and a yeoman was busy placing colored pins in the chart to mark the positions of the Combined Fleet derived from intercepted messages. There were white pins for aircraft carriers, black for battleships, red for cruisers, green for destroyers, blue for transports, yellow for submarines, and so forth. Nagumo's Striking Force was a cluster of white pins edged with black, red, and green to the northwest of Midway; Yamamoto's Main Body was mainly composed of black pins with a touch of white, red, and green still farther off to the northwest; and the Occupation Force appeared mainly as blue pins with an outer circle of red and green to the southwest. Finally, two lines of yellow pins east of Midway Island, running more or less from north to south, marked the Japanese submarines' picket lines, which would ambush the Pacific Fleet as it approached.

I was seated in a recessed area formed by tables on three sides which held the IBM runs with earlier messages in the same code,

Code	Japanese	Code	Japanese	Code	Japanese	Code	Japanese
	(海軍)暗號書名		豫メ(…ヲ)準備(ス) [Ara]		(ニ)在ラズ		
45140	暗號書表	21873	豫メ(…ヲ)準備シ置(ク)	94809			
60843	暗號特技兵(…名)	17928		26937	(ニ)在リテ		
57261	暗褐色	08772		91644	(ニ)在ルガ如(シ)		
46380	暗黒(ナ>)	89463	大略(アラマシ)	54213	(ニ)在ルヤ		
78343	暗獄	09804	霞	82197	在廳		
64080	暗殺(ス)	23079	荒(ラ>レ)	32955			
14466	暗礁	86553	荒々シキ[ク]	50262			
99780	暗礁ニ觸(ルゝ)	02844	荒波	87453	有(ル>)(アヲ見ヨ)		
01611	暗闘(ス)	36657		62109	有ラユル		
53793	暗中	79740	粗(ラ>)	80730	有難(シ)		
21222	暗中摸索(ス)	35043	嵐	50457	有樣		
38523	暗夜	73839	爭(フ)	38490	有丈ケ		
54642	暗躍(ス)	66726	爭ヒ難(ヒ)	43053	有體		
41757	暗示(ス)	70005		51348			
27951		23322	新(ラ>)(Ata ヲ見ヨ)	97977			[Ari
93936	鞍	45279	新ニ	47601	或		[Ar...
60192	鞍部	13752		79476	或ハ		
98352	譜	21471	更(ス)	84681	或日		
62859	諸藤(ス)	06732	更メテ	71313	或方面		
74103	闇	35016	改(ム)	66591	或信ズベキ		
93597	孔	13404	改マ(ル)	41406	或筋		
89892	穴	99747	改メラレ[ル][ンン]	59799	或確ナル		
44307	俺(ゝゝ)	38949	改メラルル豫定(サルゝ)	12957	或程度		
18948	強チ	71205	改メテ	82725	或點		
26667	姉[姉]	56811	改ムル	74760	或時		
11322	兄	08022		33444	或處		
80214	堂	78534	陽ハニ	21798	或夜		
00798	堂計ラン(ヤ)	08973	表ハ(ス)	97827	或時機		
55734	青 (Sei ヲ見ヨ) [Ao]	16116	表ハ(ス)	19272			
12774	青赤	88029	表ハレズ[ザル]	89061	麻		[Asa]
63291	青軍	45393		78105	朝		
11319	青空	92316	現ハ(ス)	93588	朝日		
88560	青寫眞(…枚)	47118	現ハ(ス)	19116	朝香宮		
50667	仰(ス)	83595	現ハサズ[ザル]	64620			
46599	仰向(ク)	71817		27378	旭		
30132	燗(ス)	39876	著ハ(ス)	92496	淺(ス>ク)		
13731	天晴	11493	露ハ(ス)	47820	淺々(ス)		
76107	洗(ヒ) [Ara]	00852	顯ハ(ス)	78339	淺野		
40044	豫メ	26040	非ズ[ザル](アヲ見ヨ)	47037	淺瀬		
74391	豫メ	80217	荒(ス)(Araヲ見ヨ)	90291			
34848	豫メ(…ノ)許可(スル)	26154	荒模樣	05106	汗		[Ase]
85980	豫メ(…ト)協議	90300		20691	焦(ス)		
42726	豫メ(…ヲ)承知	86187	(ニ在)(アヲ見ヨ) [Ari]	86808	足		
75390	豫メ(…ト)打合(ス)	38253	(ニ在ラバ)	78489	足場		
60525	アリ	82617	ナシ	91911	ニ依リ	43125	セリ

9. A page from a captured Japanese code book, showing five-digit code groups and their equivalents in Japanese.

the space behind my chair remaining open. The table directly in front of me had room for baskets containing the incoming messages and various reference books that I liked to have close at hand. Among other books I made frequent use of the Rose-Innes *Dictionary of Chinese-Japanese Characters* and Kenkyusha's Japanese-English and English-Japanese dictionaries as well as a book of Japanese naval terms. Somehow the room seemed more crowded than usual as people came and went and we received messages in a steady stream from our intercept stations. What we had found thus far, however, offered little comfort. The general impression was that the Japanese forces were brushing aside any opposition they encountered. A curtain of gloom hung over the room in which I sat with the other cryptanalysts. Occasionally I glanced over at Mason, who was nervously pacing about the room but, for once, had stopped yelling for coffee.

Most of the incoming messages that originated from Nagumo's Mobile Fleet reported air attacks but claimed that there had not been any damage. Suddenly there came the report of an attack by an enemy submarine: two torpedoes, no hits! We felt all the more frustrated because our side knew what to expect and yet inexplicably had failed to inflict damage, if such reports were to be believed. Sitting far away in Washington, we kept waiting impatiently and anxiously for the Japanese version of events, however unreliable that might be.

Again there came a flurry of messages that we could read without difficulty. Attacks this time by carrier-based torpedo planes—obviously from one of Spruance's three carriers in the area—but with equally dismal results. Supposedly the whole flight of sixteen planes had been shot down. No damage to the Japanese ships!

After a short interval a young redheaded yeoman rushed in with a new message. I looked at it with a shiver of excitement. The message came from the fleet carrier *Akagi* with Nagumo's force. Another attack, this time by dive bombers. Obviously our carriers had moved into range and were throwing everything at the Mobile Fleet. But the tone of the messages had changed. *Akagi* had not

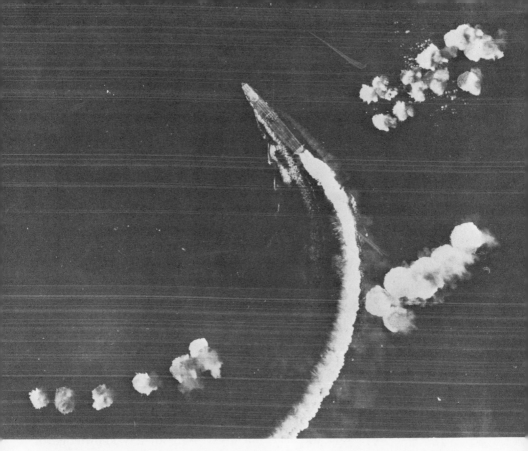

10. The Japanese carrier *Akagi* under fire by dive bombers at the Battle of Midway, June 4, 1942. Photo was taken from a U.S. bomber at an altitude of 20,000 feet.

escaped unscathed; her captain reported that the carrier was on fire.

I turned to look for Mason, but he was already standing behind me and snatched the message out of my hand.

"Good—good," he muttered and hurried off, taking the message with him.

While he was gone, I received a new batch of messages. The tone of these messages, like the first one from *Akagi*, conveyed extreme alarm and shock. When I looked at the first of these messages, I thought it had to be a duplicate of the *Akagi* message I had just read and passed to Mason. But this came from the carrier

Kaga. Almost word for word, it reported the same alarming news: *Kaga* had received direct hits from dive bombers and was ablaze.

Incredible as it seemed, the very next message repeated the same details. Attacks by torpedo planes and dive bombers. The ship was on fire. Yet again it was no duplicate of previous messages. Now it was the turn of a third big carrier, *Soryu.*

I showed the decoded messages to the men standing around me just as the old man, Mason, hurried back. The unthinkable happened: hardened navy men, probably with a total of a hundred years in service, crowded around and a loud cheer went up, even Mason breaking into one of his rare grins, with the look of a toothless baby.

It was still morning at the battle scene but early evening in Washington. The latest news meant that three of Nagumo's four big carriers were damaged and on fire, leaving only *Hiryu* so far untouched. Soon word came that Nagumo was transferring his flag from the burning *Akagi* to a cruiser. Long after the event it became known that Nagumo had refused to leave the ship and was dragged off the bridge by his own officers.

But the battle was far from over. Without any knowledge of events on our side, we hardly dared to hope that our forces had suffered no losses of their own. Moreover, the tide of battle could still turn against us in view of the presence of nearly the entire Combined Fleet in the central and northern Pacific.

All through the night the message intercepts poured in. We became bleary-eyed from working under artificial lights with no sleep, but as we picked through the impressive stack of messages we found even more reason for optimism. Shortly after midnight *Hiryu*'s captain reported that his ship had shared the fate of the other carriers. Bomb hits, the ship blazing all over. Astonishing . . . The identical short message, in nearly identical language, from all four carriers—a message we had seen again and again from marus under air attack.

At this point we knew that all four carriers were still afloat, but burning. *Kaga* got off a message reporting that she had escaped a submarine attack. But any satisfaction or relief Admiral Yamamoto might have obtained from this message disappeared a short time later when Nagumo informed him that *Kaga* had been racked by internal explosions and finally sank. Nagumo was forced to send the same bad news about *Soryu*, which went down about the same time.

Yet if Yamamoto was able somehow to concentrate his forces, he still could call on substantial air support. Even without Nagumo's two other badly wounded carriers, Yamamoto had *Junyo* and *Ryujo* with Adm. Kakuji Kakuta's Aleutian group, the light carrier *Hosho* with his own Main Body of battleships, and another light carrier, *Zuiho*, with the Midway Occupation Force.

In the early morning hours in Washington we intercepted a message containing an order from CinC, Combined Fleet, which suggested that Yamamoto was far from abandoning the battle. Mason ordered me to drop everything else and concentrate on Yamamoto's message.

This took a considerable amount of digging through the IBM runs, but I succeeded in getting the gist of the message. Yamamoto asserted that the enemy fleet had been virtually destroyed, with its remnants retiring eastward, and he ordered the units under his command to pursue the retreating enemy and to occupy Midway Island.

After the lift we had gotten from the triumphs of earlier hours, we suddenly felt as if we had been plunged into the depths. Clearly our fleet, despite the damage we had inflicted on the Japanese, must have suffered very heavy, perhaps crippling, damage in return.

We did not learn until later that, in this message, Yamamoto was exaggerating Japanese successes in the battle thus far, perhaps in order to inspire and boost the morale of his men. It was true that he still had formidable strength at his disposal. He also knew something we did not know: one American carrier, *Yorktown*, had been severely damaged and possibly sunk. Yamamoto chose to order a night action in the hope that American air strength would

11. The Japanese carrier *Hiryu* burning on June 5, 1942, after attacks by U.S. planes during the Battle of Midway.

be neutralized by darkness and that in night warfare, at which the Japanese were unexcelled, his heavy surface ships could come to grips with the U.S. fleet and even sink one or both of the two remaining carriers.

As a result of Yamamoto's order, Adm. Nobutake Kondo, who had replaced the demoralized Nagumo in command of the Mobile Force, was proceeding with a force of four battleships, nine cruisers, and nineteen destroyers to seek a night action. If he made contact with Spruance's force, our worst fears might very well be realized.

Because of the American commander's prudence, this desperate Japanese effort to retrieve the situation failed. Admiral Spruance, commanding the U.S. carrier force, had wisely decided to retire to the east during the night, and Kondo failed to make contact with the elusive enemy.

Not many hours after his original order, Yamamoto sent off another order in which he canceled the Midway operation. Knowing that there were still two enemy carriers operating in the area, he feared that at daybreak his forces would be exposed to devastating air attack. All surface forces were to withdraw to the west, except for destroyers standing by the burning *Akagi* and *Hiryu*, which were still afloat but incapable of making way.

More trouble developed for the Japanese, however, when two heavy cruisers, *Mogami* and *Mikuma*, on a mission to shell Midway but now retiring in accordance with Yamamoto's latest order, spotted an American submarine and, in their frantic evasive action, collided with one another. Bob Paine, coming on duty in the morning, worked on the messages of distress from the cruisers. *Mogami*, it seemed, had sustained damage to her bow while *Mikuma* had a ruptured oil tank. Both ships could still make way and were trying desperately to move off to the west as far and as fast as possible, but their progress was slow.

GZ sent off word of the cruisers' predicament. A telltale black slick remained behind the ships drawing the hunters just as the blood of a wounded deer provides a spoor for predatory wolves. At daylight, following the slick, dive bombers from Midway easily located the cruisers and attacked. Then B-17s came over and dropped their bombs. By afternoon in Washington we received further messages from the crippled cruisers calling for help as they limped westward. But they had not been mortally wounded by these air attacks.

About the same time Japanese destroyers sent word that they had sunk the burned-out hulks of *Akagi* and *Hiryu* with torpedoes. So we knew with certainty that the four big fleet carriers constituting the muscle of Nagumo's Mobile Force at the start of the battle had all gone to the bottom in the course of two days of confused fighting.

Informed that the two damaged Japanese heavy cruisers were still afloat, Nimitz ordered renewed attacks on *Mogami* and *Mikuma*, which, with two escorting destroyers, continued to put some distance between themselves and the enemy. Spruance's carrier group composed of *Hornet* and *Enterprise* had turned westward again during the day and now was pursuing the two cruisers. Soon both cruisers sent a stream of messages reporting repeated savage attacks by carrier-based planes, favored by clear skies with excellent visibility and a smooth sea that made their launching and landing on flight decks very easy.

In due course we received a message from *Mikuma*'s captain reporting that his ship was sinking. However, *Mogami* had withstood unbelievably heavy punishment and, in spite of continual attacks, kept moving slowly in the direction of Truk to the southwest.

By evening Spruance decided that prudence called for another withdrawal to the east, and once more he made a wise decision. On this occasion Yamamoto dispatched a force of seven cruisers and eight destroyers to proceed to the assistance of *Mogami* and *Mikuma* and attack enemy forces in the area.

The Japanese continued to pin their hopes to a night action, when Yamamoto's Main Body would move south to join the engagement. Since Spruance's destroyer cover had been reduced as fuel ran low and his fliers were exhausted from three days of ceaseless action, his decision to withdraw avoided what might easily have turned out to be a disaster.

This disengagement ended the battle. The result, as it stood, was Japan's first decisive naval defeat. The Imperial Navy had lost four first-line carriers and a heavy cruiser to the U.S. Navy's loss of one aircraft carrier and one destroyer. Apart from the carriers, Japan had lost 300 planes against the United States' 150, and 3,500 Japanese had perished while 300 Americans lost their lives. Japanese manpower losses included more than 100 combat-wise pilots whose loss would be sorely felt by the Imperial Navy.

There was no pause for congratulations in GZ after the Battle of Midway ended. No one broke out the champagne. Mason quickly put an end to the air of festivity. "Let's get on with the job," he snapped, sending those engaged in postmortems of the battle back to their desks. And although the men who fought the battle deserved the highest praise, we did not even receive a

"Well done" from the chief of naval operations or anyone else.

Still, we knew without receiving commendation that everyone from the top down recognized the crucial importance of communications intelligence in winning the Battle of Midway.

As General Marshall wrote to Republican nominee Gov. Thomas E. Dewey during the 1944 presidential campaign: "The battle of the Coral Sea was based on deciphered [sic] messages and therefore our few ships were in the right place at the right time. Further, we were able to concentrate our limited forces to meet their naval advance on Midway when otherwise we almost certainly would have been some 3,000 miles out of the way. . . ."

The Japanese authorities clamped heavy censorship on all news of the battle, even after it was over. Crews returning from Midway were denied shore leave; other personnel found themselves confined in camps. The government withheld from the public any type of information about it, deleting any references in war accounts and diaries published at a later date.

No effort on the part of Japan's leaders to conceal the facts, however, could alter those facts. Imperial Japan had failed to achieve the two main objectives of the battle: the occupation of Midway Island and the destruction of the U.S. Pacific Fleet. In the process Japan had suffered severe, possibly irreparable, losses.

After the early shattering defeats of the war, we needed, on our side, to regain confidence in ourselves. Now we knew beyond doubt that we could meet the formidable Japanese naval power and win against odds. And to me at least it seemed as if midnight—in the depths of our despair when spirits were at their lowest ebb— had passed at last; although blackness remained, the streaks of dawn on the night horizon could not be far off.

CHAPTER 5

Blood-Red Sun over a Picture-Book Island

IN Washington August 6, 1942, was a sultry and apparently uneventful Thursday—sultry as only Washington could be with its subtropical climate—and, suffering from the effects of a late night out with some friends bound for Pearl Harbor, I was having a great deal of trouble concentrating on my work.

I drank almost as much coffee that day as Mason himself normally consumed, but by afternoon I found it increasingly difficult to keep my eyes open, feeling an urgent desire to nod off at my desk.

Mason prevented the worst from happening by hovering around me throughout that long day. Under normal circumstances I was not the object of much attention from him (for which I could not help being grateful), since he usually worked in the big room with the more senior cryptanalysts on communications involving the larger plans and operations of the Imperial Navy. To myself I explained his unusual interest in my work with the wry notion that time was hanging heavy on his hands because he had been tempo-

rarily deprived of anything to do in the other area. It never occurred to me that Mason might have a very definite purpose in oc-
cupying himself with me and that his interest was prompted by the
first American amphibious operation of the Pacific war—an operation about which I still knew nothing.

"What have you got?" Mason said in his gruff way, rummaging
through my In-box.

"Nothing," I said. "It's been a quiet day. I haven't seen anything of special interest."

He grimaced. "Keep looking. Be sure to come to me with anything that looks important."

"Aye, aye, sir."

I did not have to go to Mason, for he was right on the spot
when the intercepted messages started coming in. A message from
Tulagi reported: "A force of ships of unknown number and types is
approaching. What can these ships be?" Shortly thereafter the Japanese reported a heavy bombardment by enemy surface ships, followed by a terse message: "The enemy has commenced landing."
Other excited messages amplified the first message about the landing, noting that the landing force was composed of American marines. The place: Guadalcanal.

Hardly able to believe this news, I turned and handed the first
few messages to Mason. He took one look at them and rushed off.

And so it began.

Put your finger on a speck on the map. A picture-book tropical
island ninety miles long by about twenty-five miles in width, with
white sand beaches and nodding coconut palms contrasting with
the bluest of blue water. The jungle-clad mountains rise as high as
eight thousand feet in the southern part of the island, while the
northern part is a sloping plain crossed by rivers and streams, with
rain forest and coconut plantations and fields of tall grass. Despite
its romantic appearance, the island has a hot, moist, malarial climate; even at some distance out to sea it belies its tropical beauty
with a fetid stench compounded of jungle slime, mud, and rot.
Both the Japanese and the Americans who found themselves

locked in mortal combat there hated the boot-sucking, black morass in which they had somehow to exist and move and fight at the same time. Jungle vegetation restricted visibility to a few yards, and in ravines between the ridges it trapped hot, heavy air and insects as well as the unfortunate two-legged creatures who ventured into its tangled growth.

One of war's gruesome oddities brought about a situation in which this primitive island, whose prewar population barely exceeded fifteen thousand, mostly Melanesians, was to become at its peak a bloody battleground for some sixty thousand American and Japanese fighting men equipped with the most modern weapons.

Strangest of all was the fact that they should have fought there. If military minds in Japan or the United States had devoted a single minute's thought to this island in the southeastern Solomons before the war, it must have been a well-kept secret. As late as July 2, 1942, when a Joint Chiefs of Staff directive was issued, American operational plans called for seizure of the Santa Cruz Islands, Tulagi, and "adjacent positions" (making no mention of Guadalcanal) as the first phase of a U.S. counteroffensive in the south Pacific. No landing on Guadalcanal entered into these plans until aerial reconnaissance early in July disclosed that the Japanese were building an airfield there.

Earlier the Japanese themselves had planned to invade Fiji, Samoa, and New Caledonia, but this ambitious project was canceled after their defeat at Midway. Nevertheless, they decided to concentrate air power and accelerate airfield construction in the southwest Pacific; Guadalcanal, the southernmost point they had reached in that area, afforded ideal terrain for an airfield. Not only would this airfield, when constructed, protect the flank of a renewed Japanese offensive against Port Moresby, but it also provided a base for attacking shipping and cutting off communications between the United States and Australia. Eventually, from the Japanese point of view, this airfield could become the cornerstone of a new southern advance.

Thus U.S. and Japanese plans collided head-on at the small

island of Guadalcanal. Each side was determined, for defensive reasons, to prevent the other side from using the island and to make it a base for offensive operations.

Construction of the airfield on Guadalcanal, begun only toward the end of June by the Japanese, sparked an explosion that would be heard around the world and leave its mark on the history of World War II in the Pacific.

The news that reached us at that time indicated complete success of the amphibious operation: not only a virtually unopposed landing on Guadalcanal itself but also the rapid overpowering of the Japanese garrisons on Tulagi and tiny adjacent islands. While the American high command undoubtedly anticipated a prompt and violent reaction by the Japanese, in GZ we remained in the dark about enemy plans and continued to be optimistic about the further course of the operation, believing as we did that complete occupation of Guadalcanal was now to all intents and purposes a fait accompli.

In the light of subsequent events our optimism would later appear naive if not ridiculous. We had no prior knowledge that a strong Japanese naval force of five heavy cruisers, one light cruiser, and a destroyer under the command of Adm. Gunichi Mikawa was already under way in accordance with Yamamoto's orders to carry out a night attack on the invaders at Tulagi and Guadalcanal. This force sortied from Rabaul and headed for the passage through the Solomons that, as a well-traveled route for Japanese warships and transports, later became famous as the "Slot." Although an Australian plane actually sighted Mikawa's force, a warning failed to reach the Allied forces in time.

The result was the Battle of Savo Island, in the early postmidnight hours of August 9, an unmitigated disaster for the U.S. Navy, which was caught completely off guard. Masters of night warfare, Mikawa's force carried out a highly successful action, using flares and searchlights, as the Japanese went through the Allied positions like an Indian raiding party through a sleeping enemy encampment. They sank four heavy cruisers—one Australian and three

American—without loss to themselves. The only consolation for the United States was Mikawa's failure to sink the Allied transports, which were helplessly exposed; loss of the transports would have been a devastating, possibly fatal, setback for the invasion forces.

Even so, incessant air attacks forced the transports to depart the following afternoon, taking with them half of the cargo they carried in their holds. Because of this, the U.S. Marines on shore found themselves on short rations for some time to come, fortunate only in having access to great stores of rice, soy sauce, canned vegetables, and beer captured at the Japanese base on Guadalcanal.

Some good fortune came my way in the form of a gift that had been in the booty captured on the island. One morning, reporting for duty, I discovered on my desk a medium-sized volume bound in red cloth charred at the edges. It turned out to be an original copy of the code on which I was working.

As I learned later, the code book had been captured at the moment when the marines overran the airfield. One marine, more alert or curious than others, noticed a bonfire in which a number of books and papers were burning. The marine quickly salvaged those materials that remained intact, and it turned out to be an invaluable haul of secret documents.

Thus for a certain period of time I did not have to worry about recovery of code groups. As soon as we had translated the plain text, all intercepted messages came to me in complete form, except for garbled code groups, which I usually recognized at once and correctly filled in myself.

Phil Cate, with his birdlike, darting black eyes and pixieish manner, seized the opportunity to come over and tease me. "Now you can go home, Van. We won't need you anymore."

It was a strange and somewhat humbling experience, the kind of experience one might have after reconstructing in one's imagination a picture of a foreign place based on bits and pieces picked up from the accounts of travelers and then actually seeing the place with one's own eyes and finding it different in some respects from the place one had imagined. At the same time it was also possible to confirm many impressions beyond all doubt.

The opportunities that had been offered, the perspectives that could be seen far more clearly than before filled my days and occupied my mind even during the nights. Just as overhearing a conversation between people who trust one another furnishes a true insight into their thoughts and feelings, I felt that I now understood certain things about the Japanese I might not have grasped before.

They had steeled their hearts against the enemy and would destroy him (meaning us) without hesitation. There was no Christian strain of mercy in them. For all that, one could not help admiring the unshakable resolve with which they went to their deaths, or feeling sorry about their personal suffering as well as their mourning over the fates of comrades or loved ones. Their reactions were not our reactions even though human misery had a universal quality. We did not find it easy to understand them, and therefore it was harder to feel compassion for them, particularly in the face of the cruelty they could display toward others. All of this emerged from their messages and left on me an indelible impression, making me wonder whether there was some fatal flaw in man that caused him to be both pitiless and pitiable at one and the same time.

Despite these confused feelings toward our enemy, I shared with other Americans at that time an elation stemming from recent events—an elation dampened by the news that reached us of the fate of our old friend Ralph Cory.

Lt. Ralph Cory, USMCR, landed on that steamy morning of August 7 with his fellow marines on a strip of black sand west of the Tenaru River on Guadalcanal. There was little opposition, and he and his comrades soon established a defense perimeter.

Cory had less than a week to live.

By evening the landing beach was piled high with supplies. The marines endured the usual tropical rainstorm the same night and slept under palms. The next day, August 8, the combat teams advanced toward their twin objectives, the airfield and the Japanese base installations.

A call went back during the day for Cory, who was needed to interrogate the first Japanese prisoners, laborers who had been working on the airfield. After the airfield and the base had been seized, Cory remained behind while the marines resumed their advance both along the coast and inland in a westerly direction.

As the days passed, Cory had little time to think of anything but his interrogation of Japanese prisoners, including some badly wounded soldiers. Although a few prisoners were cooperative, the large majority of them refused to answer any questions.

One prisoner who had been captured in the last few hours turned out to be unusually interesting. A seaman, he answered Cory's questions reluctantly, with a surly manner. After lengthy interrogation that produced only a small amount of information, Cory offered the seaman some brandy. The prisoner drank a couple of glasses and finally, further warmed by Cory's friendliness, began to talk. He told Cory that there was a large detachment of Japanese troops at the village of Matanikau, to the west along the coast. He said that the detachment was ready to surrender, and he offered to lead the Americans to the spot.

Cory consulted with Colonel Goettge, the G2 or intelligence officer of the First Marine Division, who was his boss. Since they had received a report a little earlier to the effect that a white flag was seen on the west bank of the Matanikau River, the sailor's statement sounded reliable. Goettge rounded up a party of men, most of them, like Cory, members of his intelligence section—about twenty-five officers and men—and set out in a landing boat along the coast to the vicinity of Matanikau village.

The party of marines went ashore around midnight on a smooth sand beach near a coconut grove, but before they could move inland they were suddenly pinned down by intense fire that killed several men and seriously wounded Cory. He lay on the beach, bleeding heavily and unable to move. The Japanese fire became still more intense as the enemy, still spraying the beach with machine gun bullets, began to lob in mortar shells. Seeing the hope-lessness of the situation, a few marines decided to try to escape before it was too late. The three men plunged into the sea and swam away from the shore.

Occasionally the swimmers looked back, and at last, in the bright moonlight, they saw that the Japanese had overrun the position of the marines and were bayoneting those who still lived. One of the swimmers thought he saw a soldier thrust his bayonet into Cory's body, stretched out on the sand where he had first fallen.

The three men who escaped, swimming and wading and crawling over coral reefs that cut and lacerated them badly, were the only survivors of Colonel Goettge's party of marines. As I heard the story, I could not help wondering what would have happened if the Japanese had been in a mood to take prisoners. It seemed likely that Cory would have fallen into their hands. It would not have been long before they identified him as a Japanese language interpreter. That would have inevitably marked him as a special target for interrogation.

If Cory had been compelled to reveal his knowledge (even strong men had broken under interrogation), the Japanese would have learned about Magic, our access to their highest-level diplomatic correspondence. They would have found out that, with PUR-PLE, we had reconstructed their Type No. 97 machine. Their ignorance of this fact resulted in continued use of the Type No. 97 machine all through the war and up to its very end. And we were not restricted to Japanese secrets alone: in October 1943, fourteen months after Cory's death, Baron Oshima, the Japanese ambassador in Berlin, was allowed to tour the West Wall and the Sieg-fried Line, and we intercepted his extremely detailed report in PURPLE on the strengthening of German defenses in preparation for an Allied invasion of Europe—information of great value to the planners of that invasion.

But Cory's value to the Japanese would not have ended with the information he could have given them about the PURPLE machine. They could have also learned that we were reading the

Imperial Navy's communications, and had they done so they would have finally understood why they suffered a shattering defeat at Midway. They would have been stung into making the drastic changes in their cryptographic systems that were absolutely essential in order to avoid similar mistakes during subsequent stages of the war.

If this misfortune had befallen us, we would have owed it all to the shortsightedness or sin of omission on the part of people who, in effect, allowed Ralph Cory to fall into a Japanese ambush on Guadalcanal. How did it happen that a man with the top-secret information possessed by Cory—among the most closely held secrets of the war—had been cleared to go into a combat zone? Why did those in authority who knew Cory's background fail to foresee the potential damage to America's national interests?

Cory's personal fate, tragic as it was, did not differ from that of many other men whose lives were lost in the service of their country. But his fate could have done immense harm to our larger fortunes in war. We were luckier than we deserved to be, although poor Cory's luck had run out.

One warm evening during this time I drove with Walter Nichols in his convertible out into Virginia, where we visited Commander Kramer. We took some wrong turns and found ourselves lost in the shadow of the Pentagon, still unoccupied, a huge dark bulk surrounded by an even huger, garishly lit construction site traversed by only a few paved roads. In a while we got our bearings and made our way to Kramer's modest frame house in nearby Arlington. He was alone at home and entertained us with his usual courtesy and quiet dignity. Later as we drove back to Washington, I felt depressed by the thought that as long as people remembered the Pearl Harbor disaster Kramer would be forced to answer the same old questions.

But I had little time to dwell on the past; we were too much caught up in what was happening in the south Pacific. It became apparent very soon that the Japanese had no intention of allowing us to conquer Guadalcanal at our leisure. While the United States

had underestimated the dimensions that the struggle would assume, it was fortunate for us that the Japanese, initially at least, fell
into the same error. Grossly underestimating the strength of the
U.S. Marines who had landed on the island, they believed that
they could easily recapture their lost positions. They held the
American fighting man in low esteem. As a result, they continued
to send the bulk of their available ground forces to New Guinea to
take part in the overland drive against Port Moresby in Papua,
which was still regarded as the prime objective of Japanese operations in the south Pacific area. They began to transport some reinforcements to their men who were still holding out on Guadalcanal, but failed to commit sufficiently large forces to ensure the
success of their counterattack.

This incorrect Japanese appraisal of the situation was strengthened on or about August 10 by a message sent home through diplomatic channels by Japan's military attaché in Moscow. In that
message the military attaché reported that, according to
"well-informed" Soviet sources, the U.S. force on Guadalcanal consisted of no more than a few thousand men whose mission was to
destroy the airfield and then withdraw. The American troops, he
reported, were low in morale and in no condition to sustain a long
campaign.

In GZ we assumed that the report had been planted by Soviet
officials, probably in a typical attempt at *disinformatsiya* or "disinformation," the planting of false or misleading information designed
to conceal the true state of affairs from the target of the operation. I
certainly could not imagine what the Soviet officials hoped to
achieve by their *disinformatsiya* other than to disarm the Japanese
and perhaps slow down the pace of their conquests. Any lingering
doubts the Russians themselves might have had about the real situation were dispelled before long. On August 19 Roosevelt informed
Stalin, "We have gained, I believe, a toehold in the Southwest Pacific from which the Japanese will find it very difficult to dislodge
us. . . ."

As the Japanese campaign to reinforce their forces on Guadalcanal intensified, a first contingent of nine hundred men landed on August 21 east of the airfield but, overconfident of their strength and, perhaps more to the point, despising the American foe, they attacked prematurely and were wiped out almost to the last man.

Nevertheless, additional reinforcements were already on the way. More important, Yamamoto thought that the effort to reinforce the Japanese garrison on Guadalcanal would force the U.S. Navy to give battle and thus enable him to achieve his long-sought goal of wearing down and ultimately destroying the Pacific Fleet. Therefore he issued orders to the Combined Fleet to sortie from its base at Truk in the Carolines and engage American warships in the Solomons area while the reinforcements landed on Guadalcanal, contributing to a buildup that would overwhelm the Americans in due course.

GZ saw the last-minute messages informing the Japanese naval high command about the Combined Fleet's actual time of departure from Truk. It was one thing to know that the enemy's battleships and carriers were on the way south, however, and another thing to meet and defeat them. We could ensure that our ships and planes were in the right place at the right time, as in the case of Midway, but victory remained subject to the vagaries of chance and the caprices of human error.

Moreover, the Japanese force was at impressive strength, for it included the fleet carriers *Shokaku* and *Zuikaku*, the light carrier *Ryujo*, two battleships, four heavy cruisers, one light cruiser, and no fewer than fourteen destroyers.

Before long the Japanese detected Admiral Fletcher's task force cruising 150 miles east of Guadalcanal. Fletcher had had three carriers—*Saratoga*, *Enterprise*, and *Wasp*—with one battleship, four cruisers, and ten destroyers, but when it appeared that no naval action was immediately impending, he had sent the *Wasp* group south to refuel, thereby depriving himself of air power that might have given him a significant edge in the battle that was now about to begin.

On August 24 Fletcher's patrol planes found the enemy. Unfortunately it was not the Japanese main force but a group operating with *Ryujo* far in advance of the other ships, preparing to neutralize Henderson Field on Guadalcanal so that the transports could disembark troops without interference from the air. At the same time the big Japanese carriers launched their planes against Fletcher's force.

The first messages we received were contact reports from *Ryujo* testifying to the efficacy of American air attacks. After earlier reports of heavy damage, *Ryujo* got off a final message to Yamamoto's headquarters that she was sinking. Meanwhile the Japanese pilots concentrated their attacks on the *Enterprise* group and, in spite of fierce defensive action by our fighters, managed to deliver some direct hits on the carrier's flight deck, also knocking out two elevators.

After these exchanges the Japanese had lost one light carrier and ninety planes against the damage to *Enterprise* and the loss of only twenty American planes. Smarting under these losses, the Japanese force withdrew in the direction of Truk. While the result of this battle was inconclusive, Yamamoto had not only missed another hoped-for victory at sea but abandoned the field to the enemy.

While the battle was in progress, the Japanese transports tenaciously held to their course toward Guadalcanal, but they were subjected to increasingly heavy punishment by American pilots flying from Henderson Field.

We in GZ decoded a report that *Kinryu Maru,* one of the transports, had taken a direct bomb hit and gone down, while the light cruiser *Jintsu,* Adm. Raizo Tanaka's flagship, was hit by a bomb forward of the bridge, buckling plates, starting fires, and knocking out communications.

When it became obvious to the Japanese command that continuation of the operation could only result in total disaster, the transports were recalled, thus canceling Guadalcanal's reinforcement for the time being.

Recognizing that direct action in broad daylight, even with the covering support of the Combined Fleet, could not succeed, the Japanese high command resolved on a new approach. We saw the first evidence of this approach in several communications directing Admiral Tanaka, commander of the Reinforcement Force, to organize and take charge of *Nezumi*, or "Rat," operations whose nature and purpose were at first unclear to us.

The *nezumi* in Japanese mythology is by no means the animal that inspires abhorrence, hatred, and fear in American life. To the Japanese the *nezumi* is a wise and cunning creature much to be admired for its ability to survive and prosper under the most adverse circumstances.

As our knowledge of the *Nezumi* operations gradually took shape, we discovered that they had much in common with the traits of the animal admired by the Japanese: the ability to move stealthily and surely in darkness, to outwit the foe by eluding his most ingenious snares and defenses, to exercise unending patience in achieving ultimate goals, and to build up overwhelming strength for a breakthrough at the right time.

For Admiral Tanaka, it came down to the task of organizing swift destroyer runs of troops and supplies to Guadalcanal at night. The destroyers lay up in the northwest Solomons out of range of most of our planes until darkness fell, then sailed at top speed down the Slot, unloaded at Guadalcanal around midnight, and returned home before daylight, unseen by the enemy. These operations, collectively dubbed the Tokyo Express by the Americans, proved to be extremely effective in building up Japanese strength on the island to a point where the Imperial Army seriously threatened the American marines ably led by Gen. Alexander Vandegrift.

While the reinforcement was going on, the Japanese high command planned a series of night bombardments of Henderson Field by heavy naval units to be coordinated with a ground offensive. The bombardments were designed to smash the airfield's runways and installations, destroy planes, fuel, and as many flight personnel as possible, thus depriving the U.S. ground forces of local air support.

12. Admiral Raizo Tanaka, Imperial Japanese Navy, in command of the Reinforcement Force.

Unfortunately, even though we had the information, there was little that Admiral Nimitz and his commanders could do to interfere with, or prevent, the Japanese from carrying out their plans. By night, thanks to their superiority in nocturnal warfare, the Imperial Navy controlled the seas around Guadalcanal; by day, American air superiority assured the U.S. Navy's mastery of the sea in that area unless Yamamoto was prepared to challenge U.S. control of the air with his big carriers, something he remained reluctant to do after Midway, except when the stakes were large enough. Later, the U.S. Navy would learn to use radar effectively and gain a tactical advantage that shifted the balance of power in night warfare decisively in our favor.

By the end of August the Japanese had also realized that they must change their priorities. A directive of the Imperial General Headquarters dated August 31, 1942, read: "First priority will be given to the immediate recapture of Guadalcanal." This decision led, a few weeks later, to the recall of Japanese troops already within sight of Port Moresby, thereby ending the overland campaign across the Papuan peninsula which seemed about to be crowned with success. The forces freed from this campaign were to be thrown into the battle for Guadalcanal.

After our marginal victory in the Battle of the Eastern Solomons, the U.S. Navy suddenly encountered, in September, some severe and depressing setbacks. *Enterprise* was already out of action owing to damage suffered in the last battle; now a Japanese submarine got a torpedo hit on *Saratoga*, removing her from the lists for three crucial months; and as if this was not bad enough, another enemy submarine sank *Wasp*. With the loss of these carriers, we were left for a time with only one U.S. carrier, *Hornet*, still operational in the south Pacific.

During this period OP-20-G had to contend with a move to new quarters in Northwest Washington where a former girls' school, the Mount Vernon Academy, with its extensive grounds had been requisitioned for navy use. Soon we moved out to our new quarters, being housed first in the brick, ivy-covered main building of the school. There was also a handsome chapel with Greek columns which would subsequently become notable because of the many navy weddings that took place there.

When I had the mid watch, I sat at an open window without a screen (there was no air-conditioning), in a low-ceilinged room on the second floor, once a classroom, trying very hard to concentrate on the IBM runs as bugs flew in from the nearby woods and hit me in the face. Aside from their enormous size, the bugs were so grotesque that I could have sworn I had never seen their like in all my life. They were of all colors, sizes, and shapes, making one wonder where nature had found some of its designs. Had I been an entomologist, I would have doubtless made some new discoveries, or so I thought. But their main function, it seemed, was to keep me awake.

In the following months a new and modern brick office building sprang up behind the original girls' school. Its modern, no-nonsense style detracted from the earlier, more charming surroundings, but we badly needed the additional space. The establishment of the Naval Communications Annex, as it was then called, at Massachusetts and Nebraska avenues, N.W., hardly slowed the pace of our work, and its presence, despite lights that blazed all night, was spared unwanted attention by the press, most notably by the famous columnist David Lawrence, who lived in a spacious tree-shaded house directly opposite the annex on Nebraska Avenue.

This was the time when the big wartime expansion of OP-20-G really began. GZ itself received a considerable number of newcomers, most of them from the Navy Language School at Boulder but a few others directly from the academic world as well as other parts of the U.S. government.

One newcomer temporarily assigned to GZ was a Foreign Service officer, Bill Turner, a sandy-haired, modest, scholarly man who had been second secretary in Tokyo under Ambassador Grew and evidently enjoyed the esteem of his chief. He had just been repatriated in August with Grew and other interned Americans on the *Gripsholm.*

Another newcomer was Lt. Col. Banks Holcomb, USMC, a nephew of Gen. Thomas Holcomb, commandant of the Marine Corps. A stocky, friendly man with wavy black hair, Banks was primarily a Chinese linguist. He had been stationed in Chungking, the remote city in Szechwan beyond the gorges of the Yangtze River, to which the Nationalist regime had withdrawn before the

Japanese advance deep into China and which became its temporary capital.

Holcomb was assigned by Mason to handle aspects of GZ's work that had a Chinese connection. At one point later on in the war Holcomb interviewed some people to fill a spot as liaison officer in Chungking. One of those interviewed for the job, an eager applicant, was tall, shy Ki Cammann, marked by a Lincoln-esque ungainliness, who had gone through the Japanese course at Harvard. Ki's first love, however, was China, and when he heard the job was open he immediately put in a bid.

After his meeting with Holcomb, Cammann met a few of us and described his interview. "I told him," Cammann said, "that I was willing to work with the Nationalist government, but I would have absolutely nothing to do with Tai Li."

Someone groaned at mention of this name. Tai Li was Chiang Kai-shek's secret police chief, who, by all accounts, was a thoroughly wicked and unscrupulous man. He would die, little mourned, in a plane crash in 1946.

"My God, didn't you know that the job calls for working with Tai Li and his people?"

Cammann did not get the liaison assignment, although he would have refused it anyway, had it been offered. But the incident reflected the central dilemma of U.S. relations with dictatorial, repressive, sometimes corrupt regimes. During World War II American leaders tended to present all such regimes to the public as "democratic" Allies, for example, the Soviet Union and Nationalist China. Roosevelt extended his favor to such regimes because they were at war with our enemies, Nazi Germany and Japan. At the same time he and other top officials in the U.S. government overlooked the fact that their objectives often differed sharply from our own. A more sober view of these regimes might have concluded that, while *assistance* was in our national interest, *alliance* was to be avoided.

In the case of Chiang Kai-shek, there was a disposition to hoard the arms and other supplies we were generously shipping, at great cost and hardship, the airplanes we flew in, the pilots and technicians we were training for the purpose of fighting the Japanese; to avoid combat at all costs; and to retreat ever deeper into the hinterland of China. Chiang was content to let the United States fight the war with Japan; he was preserving his own strength—so he believed—to fight the civil war against the Communists after the other war had ended. If there was any awareness of this in Washington, there could have been scant solace in the behavior of the Chinese Communists, who were pursuing a similar policy in areas under their control.

In another period and place Banks Holcomb would be haunted by his personal Chungking experience. During the Korean War, in December 1950, in the course of General MacArthur's "Home-by-Christmas" drive to the Yalu River, Holcomb was serving with the First Marine Division (of Guadalcanal fame) which had been cut off and surrounded by hordes of Chinese troops at Chosin Reservoir. The marines, in freezing arctic cold, suffering from hunger, frostbite, battle fatigue, and wounds, with equipment malfunctioning in the subzero temperatures, had to fight their way out of the Chinese trap over snowy, ice-slicked, narrow mountain roads or be annihilated. When Chinese prisoners were brought in, Holcomb interrogated them, trying to learn the disposition and strength of their units, which had been cunningly concealed from the Americans by movements confined to darkness and camouflage. To his shock, one Chinese prisoner said to him, "Don't you know me, Colonel?" Then Holcomb recognized the man as one whom he had frequently met in Chungking and who knew *him* well as an intelligence officer. Later, after the First Marine Division escaped, Holcomb was very happy that their positions had not been reversed.

In some cases, the newcomers in GZ brought valuable expertise with them, but as a general rule we simply needed more hands to cope with the increasing burden of traffic, the bulk of it concerned with Guadalcanal. With the help of Japanese reporting on the *Nezumi* and other transport operations we could monitor their troop buildup, which had reached six thousand by mid-September. Unimpressive as it sounded, that figure would be boosted dramatically before the struggle was over. Meanwhile the U.S. Navy, staggering from its carrier losses in the second half of September, was scraping the bottom of the barrel to find reinforcements and supplies for the marines on Guadalcanal. Admirals King and Nimitz sought vainly to appeal against commitments made by President Roosevelt, General Marshall, Gen. Henry Arnold, and other top military leaders to send every available man and plane to support the Allied landings in North Africa scheduled for November. In Washington there was growing doubt that the American forces could hold out on the island.

Preparing for a big ground offensive in October, the Japanese continued their buildup. We found in decoded messages evidence of the projected movement of the Sendai Division and the displacement to Guadalcanal of the headquarters of the Seventeenth Army under Gen. Harukichi Hyakutake, previously located at Rabaul. To weaken further the American defensive capabilities the Japanese sent a bombardment group of three cruisers and two destroyers to shell Henderson Field.

Although we had advance knowledge that they were coming, it took some good fortune this time to enable a similar force of cruisers and destroyers commanded by Admiral Scott to surprise the enemy force and gain revenge for our earlier disastrous defeat at Savo Island. When the shooting was over, soon after midnight, one Japanese cruiser, *Aoba,* had been sunk and a second one, *Kinugasa,* badly damaged. The United States lost only one destroyer in the engagement.

Two nights later, however, a couple of Japanese battleships, *Kongo* and *Haruna,* sailed into Ironbottom Sound and battered Henderson Field with their fourteen-inch guns. After such a heavy bombardment few planes remained operational to attack a convoy of transports that, on October 15, disembarked another forty-five hundred troops together with artillery on the island. In little more than a month the Japanese had raised their total strength to twenty-two thousand, most of them fresh troops, opposing twenty-three thousand Americans, battle weary and suffering severely from malaria and dysentery.

Thus another major battle at sea, on land, and in the air was in the making. As we discerned in communications intelligence, Yamamoto now meant to complete the job, planning to support the imminent big ground drive, which the Japanese hopefully envisaged as the "final solution" of the Guadalcanal situation, with the largest naval force assembled since Midway. As soon as the Imperial Army had captured the airfield, carrier planes would fly in and start operating from the field. Once the Japanese had turned the situation around and gained local control of the air, the days of the Americans on Guadalcanal would be numbered.

On October 16 we decoded one message giving details of an air attack scheduled for the next morning on Henderson Field by Japanese land-based bombers: number and types of planes, approach path, the time of attack. Cincpac forwarded the information to Guadalcanal, and U.S. fighters were in the air when the Japanese bombers arrived. Most of the attackers were shot down and the attack was repulsed.

But this was merely an incident to be quickly forgotten in the face of more critical events. When we intercepted and read orders for the impending sortie of the Combined Fleet, Nimitz arranged to have repairs rushed on *Enterprise*, as he had done once before in the case of *Yorktown* at the time of Midway, and sent her back posthaste to the battle area.

Thus, while Admiral Kondo's force of carriers and battleships was moving down from Truk, Adm. William Halsey dispatched the *Hornet* and *Enterprise* groups to the northeast of Guadalcanal, in the open sea.

Savage fighting was already in progress on the island as Japanese troops launched a surprise attack from the south out of tangled, nearly impenetrable jungle—where no foe was expected—and came close to overrunning the airfield. U.S. Marines and soldiers heroically held their positions on the grassy ridges south of the airfield, finally stalling the Japanese attack. After the Imperial Army command had notified Kondo several times to approach and send in his planes to land on the airfield, only to postpone the operation each time, Yamamoto lost patience, informing the army that Kondo was running low on fuel and, unless the airfield was captured in the next hours, he would have to order withdrawal of the naval force.

Still, Halsey meant to have a battle, and a battle there was. Kondo had already turned north away from Guadalcanal when Halsey ordered an immediate attack. The first intimation we in GZ had of what was going on came in the contact reports from Kondo's force as the first wave of our planes hit the enemy.

Early in the morning (local time) on October 26 the light carrier *Zuiho* sent off a message to the effect that carrier-based planes had swarmed over her and damaged her flight deck with two bomb hits.

Later the fleet carrier *Shokaku* reported that she was trying to evade persistent attacks by other carrier planes. *Shokaku* seemed to be an ill-fated ship; in the Battle of the Coral Sea, in May, she suffered bomb hits on her flight deck, was unable to recover her planes, and remained out of action for months. Now *Shokaku* received three direct bomb hits, one in the operations room, and her returning planes had to land on *Zuikaku*. Once again she would be out of action for many months. During the same attack the heavy cruiser *Chikuma* was also crippled.

We felt disappointed, however, that none of Kondo's ships had gone to the bottom. Our disappointment grew when we learned that, during the exchanges of air strikes, *Hornet* had been less fortunate. Listing and ablaze, dead in the water, she was finally abandoned both by her crew and by U.S. destroyers after they failed to sink her.

Yamamoto was eager to get his hands on *Hornet* and ordered his destroyers to tow her to Truk if possible. Presumably he would have liked to tow her in triumph as a war trophy into Tokyo Bay. This was not to be. By the time the Japanese destroyers reached her, *Hornet* lay so low in the water that it was only a matter of time before she went down. On the afternoon of October 27 one of Yamamoto's destroyers delivered the coup de grace with four Long Lance torpedoes, finally sinking her.

At least Yamamoto could take satisfaction from the fact that the Imperial Navy had won a tactical victory in this latest battle. He had also gained revenge for the raid on Tokyo by sinking the carrier that had launched Doolittle's bombers. Nevertheless, damage to Japanese carriers made it unlikely that they would be able to take part in later stages of the struggle for Guadalcanal. Kondo had lost one hundred planes to the seventy-five lost by Adm. Thomas Kinkaid, and this also had a negative aspect from the Japanese point of view: Japan could not match the spectacular American program for training new pilots and building planes, so the Japanese air arm was becoming progressively weaker than the American.

On the ground the Imperial Army, hitherto so certain of its invincibility, had been beaten off with heavy losses—some two thousand dead—about ten times the losses suffered by the American soldiers and marines. Yet at this point both sides were in desperate shape, afflicted not only by constant battle casualties but also by disease and hunger. Both sides were also short of ammunition and anxious for replacement of all types of arms and equipment as well as spare parts.

As the most critical phase of the Guadalcanal struggle approached in November, I suddenly obtained badly needed help myself. In addition to Bob Paine, I now had four new officers from the language school at Boulder and a chief yeoman assigned to work under my command. The new people assigned to work in the section would make it a great deal easier to cope with the flood of messages, which we could read in their entirety thanks to the captured code book, and under the pressure of time, which, as always, played a critical part in our work.

While I had to deal with these internal problems, the American high command was trying to decide whether it would continue to fight for Guadalcanal in view of the ever-mounting threat by the Japanese to annihilate our forces. In GZ we did not know that the whole campaign hung in the balance, depending on the way the decision went. Our attention was riveted on the next Japanese moves.

Then President Roosevelt intervened personally. He had originally made the agreement with Churchill to give first priority to the European war. Now, however, he became deeply concerned about the situation on Guadalcanal. Noting the reluctance of the Joint Chiefs of Staff to allocate resources to the southwest Pacific area, he addressed a memorandum to the JCS on October 24 in which he stated that he was anxious to hold Guadalcanal and to see that all necessary planes, weapons, and personnel were provided to make this effort successful.

Meanwhile the Tokyo Express speeded up its operations, bringing reinforcements nightly to Guadalcanal until, finally, the Japanese forces actually outnumbered the Americans. But this was not all. Tanaka's Reinforcement Force was preparing to transport over thirteen thousand men in eleven ships escorted by a like number of destroyers in order to obtain clear numerical superiority. As before, battleships and cruisers were to bombard Henderson Field while Kondo's carrier force, under orders from Yamamoto to avoid another battle, maneuvered well to the north and provided air cover.

Thus at the beginning of November we in GZ read the intercepted messages with growing dismay, noting some familiar but alarming signs: the sortie of the Combined Fleet from Truk, the concentration of other combat ships at Rabaul, the assembling of transports, and a buildup of land-based air strength in New Britain and the Shortlands. We wondered about the response on our side.

Unknown to us, Admiral Halsey had not been idle. He stripped the outer islands of all available forces to reinforce Guadalcanal with about six thousand men. He also prepared to meet Japanese naval power with all the American might he could bring to bear. Even the *Enterprise*, damaged again in the battle that re-

sulted in the sinking of *Hornet*, had been hastily patched up and
sent back to sea with a jammed forward elevator. President Roosevelt's personal intervention also meant that additional cruisers, destroyers, and submarines would arrive eventually in the south Pacific. Speedier help could be expected from the bombers and
fighters being rushed from bases in Australia and Hawaii.

In the midst of these developments we heard the news of the
landing in North Africa of Allied forces commanded by Gen.
Dwight D. Eisenhower. Cheered as we were by the good news,
those of us who were concerned with the Pacific war had little time
or inclination to think about anything but our own immediate problems.

We kept watching the incoming traffic with fear and trep-
idation. Suddenly the contact reports started to come in, as they
always did, in a rush. It was a moonless night over Guadalcanal,
with faint light from the stars, when the Japanese Bombardment
Group with the battleships *Hiei* and *Kirishima* approached to knock
out Henderson Field once again. This time they encountered a
force of cruisers and destroyers under Adm. William Callaghan in
the sinister black waters of Ironbottom Sound, which owed its
name to an already well-earned reputation as a graveyard of ships.

In the incredible free-for-all that now ensued, more reminiscent of the Spanish Armada than a modern sea battle, the opposing
naval forces slugged it out toe to toe. Fortunately for the Americans, the two Japanese battleships had been armed for a shore
bombardment and therefore did not carry armor-piercing shells,
which would have blown the American ships out of the water. At
such close quarters, as the ships of both sides fell out of formation
and grappled with enemy ships in individual duels, each side fired
on its own ships as well as those of the enemy, and both sides suffered grievous injury.

Only one of thirteen American cruisers and destroyers escaped
without damage; those ships that did not sink were in no condition
to continue the battle. Admiral Callaghan was killed. But the Japanese also absorbed a fearful pounding—especially the battleship

Hiei, hit by countless shells, somewhere between fifty and one hundred of them.

Through the long night the captain of *Hiei* sent out messages of distress. Reading those messages, I could not help feeling sorry for him and his ship. *Hiei* gave her position north of Savo Island again and again, as if anyone could come to her help. Blazing from stem to stern, her steering knocked out, she kept going around and around in circles in the vicinity of that unlovely island, thrusting up like the head of a Loch Ness monster out of blood-tinted inky seas.

We wasted no time in sending word that *Hiei* was still afloat, and in the morning bombers took off from nearby Henderson Field for the kill. There was no way for the unfortunate *Hiei* to escape or even defend herself, and after a cruel battering the battleship rolled over and went down.

Despite all this, Tanaka's transports retired only temporarily. The next night another Bombardment Group of cruisers commanded by Admiral Mikawa succeeded in shelling Henderson Field, then pulled back to escape from American air power at daybreak. At the same time, that courageous and tenacious Japanese admiral, Tanaka, started down the Slot again to try to effect landings on Guadalcanal.

Neither Admiral Mikawa's Bombardment Group, desperately trying to withdraw the next day, nor Admiral Tanaka's Reinforcement Force, venturing into the lion's den, escaped punishment by American planes. That next day, November 14, planes from *Enterprise* and from Henderson Field as well as B-17s from Espiritu Santo seemed to be everywhere, flying over the enemy like avenging angels.

One of Mikawa's cruisers was sunk and three others damaged. Meanwhile Tanaka's transports, which had been left virtually unprotected except for a few destroyers, came under devastating bombing attacks. One transport after the other reported that she was sinking, until by nightfall seven transports, each carrying about a thousand soldiers, had gone down.

The ultimate absurdity was that another force under Admiral

Kondo made up of the battleship *Kirishima,* which had escaped the fate of *Hiei* on the first day of the Battle of Guadalcanal, four cruisers, and nine destroyers headed down the Slot on that third night, supposedly to protect the transports (most of which had already been sunk) and to carry out a more intense bombardment of Henderson Field.

Once again the drama of a deadly, almost point-blank, shoot-out took place in the dark between heavy fleet units. This time the United States had two battleships, *South Dakota* and *Washington,* to provide a really big wallop. The messages that we received now were practically a replay of the ones we had seen from *Hiei,* as *Kirishima* came under the concentrated fire of our battleships. Shattered, burning, out of control, *Kirishima* turned in circles, and there was nothing left for her crew to do but scuttle her. So *Kirishima* met her end, joining a destroyer that had been likewise scuttled by her crew.

These setbacks did not stop the redoubtable Admiral Tanaka. He held stubbornly to the same course with his remaining four transports and ran them up on the beach at Guadalcanal, where they were able to disembark troops and supplies. However, the heavy losses suffered in these engagements discouraged the Imperial Navy from risking any more capital ships in the Solomons area. Tanaka continued his destroyer supply runs to Guadalcanal, using drums filled with supplies that were pushed overboard offshore to be retrieved by ground forces while the destroyers rushed back to their bases.

At the end of November a U.S. force of cruisers and destroyers set out to stop these operations but reckoned without the formidable seamanship of Admiral Tanaka. His destroyers were engaged in escorting transports, but Tanaka ordered the destroyers to let the transports shift for themselves and attacked the American force without hesitation. Not only did the reinforcements get ashore, but Tanaka sank one cruiser and damaged three others, losing only one destroyer of his own.

Despite his heroic efforts, American air power in the area had become much too formidable even for Tanaka's swift destroyer force. Radar also altered the balance of power in favor of the Americans, for planes from Henderson Field and PT boats operating out of Tulagi were now a serious menace at night as well as by day.

Yamamoto's solution was to have resupply operations carried out by submarines that traveled underwater during daylight and surfaced only at night off Cape Esperance on Guadalcanal to unload their supplies. The U.S. planes and ships equipped with radar, however, proved to be just as great a menace to the submarines, twenty of which were lost in the course of these operations.

This last phase of Japanese resupply and transport operations also had an unexpected denouement for U.S. communications intelligence.

It happened toward the very end of the Guadalcanal struggle, one night when a Japanese cargo-carrying submarine surfaced off the beach after having made the usual underwater run to the island during daylight hours. Too late, the captain spotted the ghostly shape of a New Zealand corvette that was patrolling in that sector.

Events unfolded in jerky scenes as in a badly cut film: The corvette charging down upon the surfaced submarine, firing deck guns and even torpedoes . . . The submarine desperately trying to dive . . . An explosion that knocks out the submarine's power and leaves the crew in total blackness . . . The captain decides to surface again . . . He and his gun crew shoot back at the corvette but are cut down by machine gun fire . . . The corvette rams the submarine . . . The submarine's navigator with sword held high, hoarsely shouting, tries to board the corvette but loses his footing and falls into the sea . . . The stricken submarine slowly settling at a shallow depth to remain with her bow pointing out of the water like the accusing arm of a drowned man . . .

Eventually U.S. Navy divers would extract from the submarine wreckage a haul of Japanese secret communications materials—too late to be of use for the climax at Guadalcanal.

By this time I had bid farewell to Sy Millstein, who had received his orders to proceed to Brisbane, Australia. I felt the loss

13. U.S. intelligence officers question a Japanese prisoner captured on Guadal-canal in January 1943.

keenly, as I loved him like an older brother. Sy had been assigned to Adm. Daniel Barbey's staff with the Amphibious Force, whose mission was to support General MacArthur's southwest Pacific campaign.

Both strong personalities, Admiral King and General MacArthur once again clashed—as they would repeatedly on other occasions—over Pacific strategy. Both men wanted a unified command in the Pacific, but King wanted to give the command to Nimitz while MacArthur wanted it for himself. Since agreement on a unified command therefore seemed out of the question, each man strove to divert the lion's share of available resources to his own theater. At the same time, each argued for his own objective: MacArthur demanded that priority be given for a drive aimed at the formidable base of Rabaul, while King pushed hard for a central Pacific campaign.

This tug-of-war continued in Allied military councils and among the Joint Chiefs of Staff, but in a less rarefied atmosphere few of us thought about future strategy, little suspecting how short a time was left in the Guadalcanal campaign. While we remained far from confident about the outcome, Imperial General Headquarters had already decided that the Japanese position on the island was hopeless. Although they still had fifty thousand troops waiting at Rabaul, the Japanese commanders could find no way to move them to Guadalcanal because the United States controlled the area so thoroughly in the air and at sea that any transports venturing down the Slot were sure to be sunk.

On the first day of the new year of 1943, the Japanese made changes in their secret communications. My original code book was no longer in use, and I had to start all over breaking into a new code book. Precisely at that time, at the beginning of January, the Japanese high command confronted the bitter truth and decided to abandon Guadalcanal, but for once their decision remained secret from us. Their plans matured without our knowledge, accompanied by some cleverly deceptive maneuvers to mislead us.

Admiral Kondo made several feints with his Combined Fleet in the direction of the southern Solomons, while transports assembled at Rabaul and in the upper Solomons, and destroyer escorts appeared on the scene. These moves were indispensable for evacuating the island, but, learning of the movements, Halsey began to wonder whether still another massive reinforcement was impending as a prelude to one more big offensive. His concern about a new offensive was heightened when a tough battalion of Japanese marines landed at Cape Esperance and started attacking in the direction of Henderson Field.

This was exactly what the Japanese wanted us to think at just the moment they were beginning their withdrawal. During the third week of January Japanese destroyers started embarking troops. By the time it was over, thirteen thousand Japanese soldiers had been evacuated without interference from the Americans, who had fixed their attention elsewhere. Six months to the day from the American landing on Guadalcanal, on February 7, 1943, the last Japanese fighting man left the island.

Needless to say, we were chagrined by the ease with which the Japanese had deceived us. If we had realized in time what was happening, we could have opened an all-out offensive and turned the evacuation into a debacle. In GZ we felt genuine regret at the opportunity that had been lost, if only because we had failed to break the intercepted messages. We knew all too well that those Japanese troops would live to fight another day.

Those Who Dwell in the Dust

O N an April evening in 1943 I read the decoded message
that was in effect the death warrant of Adm. Isoroku
Yamamoto, Japan's foremost military leader.

It has been said that in the heart of every Japanese there sleeps
a samurai. This truism applied with particular force to Admiral
Yamamoto. As a boy, he had been told many stories by his father
about their samurai ancestors, members of the Echigo clan who
had fought fierce battles on behalf of the clan against forced unifica-
tion of Japan under the Emperor Meiji.

One of the old stories the young Isoroku must have heard, a
tale known to all Japanese, was about the forty-seven *ronin.* Their
feudal lord, Asano, felt that he had been humiliated by the Grand
Chamberlain Kira and, enraged, drew his sword and slightly in-
jured Kira. The action helped Asano to regain face, but since he
had bared his sword against a superior he was forced to atone for
his action by committing ceremonial suicide. After Asano's death
his forty-seven retainers met with that saddest of fates in feudal
Japan: they became *ronin,* leaderless samurai. The forty-seven

ronin swore a solemn oath to avenge their lord's death by killing the grand chamberlain. They resorted to many tricks and subterfuges to throw Kira off guard and finally launched a surprise attack, breaking into his house and killing him. Then they cut off the grand chamberlain's head and placed it on Asano's tomb. Recognizing that the murder could not go unpunished, all forty-seven *ronin* committed suicide by disembowelment. Later generations showed their deep respect by making pilgrimages to the graves where the *ronin* lay buried side by side.

Loyalty. Honor. Courage. Self-sacrifice. The qualities Japanese parents wanted to instill in their children. But there was considerably more to the samurai than that. The code drafted by a renowned sixteenth-century general used the following words: "A man born a samurai should live and die sword in hand. Unless he is thus trained in time of peace, he will be useless in the hour of stress. To be brave and warlike must be his invariable condition."

Like the forty-seven *ronin*, the samurai schooled himself to regard death by his own hand as nothing abhorrent but rather a natural outcome. The samurai expected to be killed in battle, but if he faced capture by a victorious enemy, he took the honorable course of committing ceremonial suicide. He accomplished this by disemboweling himself, but if at the last his hand faltered, a friend stood ready with a sword to decapitate him immediately.

Apart from death in battle against the enemy or suicide to redeem his honor, the samurai of both the feudal period and the modern era might be killed at any time by his own countrymen who saw him as a menace to the larger interests of the clan or country.

The samurai was prepared to meet death not only by tradition and education but also through the transcendental influence of Buddhism. Achieving the higher mental state of absorption into a consciousness far beyond his own worldly concerns, he discovered in Buddha an eternal truth where neither life nor death, growth nor decay, existed, and he acquired an indifference to the fate that lay in store for him.

DEADLY MAGIC

Admiral Yamamoto was such a man. A man of action, not a scholar, but at the same time a keen thinker and strategist. He could easily have been killed in his very first battle, serving under Togo in the victory over the Russians at Tsushima Strait. If the occasion had ever called for it, he would unhesitatingly have died by his own hand. And he knew all too well that he could meet a similar fate at the hands of his countrymen.

He had seen this kind of event unfold more than once, most dramatically perhaps in an outbreak that the Japanese called the "February 26 Incident."

In Tokyo on the morning of February 26, 1936, a small group of extremist officers, none higher than the rank of captain, carried out a revolt aimed at getting rid of elder statesmen who, in the officers' view, were exerting a restraining influence on the emperor. For days before the revolt the officers had led their men in ostensible training exercises. Once again on February 26 the soldiers thought that they were engaged in an exercise when they surrounded a number of designated houses inside and outside the city. But it was to kill certain occupants that the officers entered each house.

At the premier's official residence, which was surrounded in this manner, the officers had less success than elsewhere, mistaking the premier's brother-in-law, Colonel Matsuo, for Admiral Okada and killing him while the premier hid and later managed to reach a safe place.

At other houses the officers shot to death Viscount Adm. Makoto Saito, a former prime minister, and Gen. Jotarō Watanabe, director of military education; fatally stabbed Finance Minister Korekiyo Takahashi; and seriously wounded Adm. Kantarō Suzuki, grand chamberlain to the emperor, by shooting him in the chest. (Suzuki, whom the mutinous officers regarded as a moderate, would recover from his wound and become the premier of Japan's last World War II government, which concluded the surrender in 1945.)

Attempts to kill other prominent statesmen failed, but the rebels remained in control of the premier's residence and the

Sanno Hotel (which would become a U.S. Army VIP billet during the postwar occupation), close to the center of Tokyo, for several days before surrendering. The officers who led the abortive revolt disappointed the public when only one of them followed the tradition of the samurai by committing ceremonial suicide. The others were dismissed from the army—an unusually severe punishment for those days, although some of them were reported condemned and executed at a later date.

A few years later Yamamoto himself was to face the threat of assassination because he opposed the policy of waging war against the United States. Yamamoto believed that Japan was certain to be defeated in such a war. Fully aware of the danger to his life, he left a note behind to be opened after his death: "I regard it as a great honor to die for what I consider to be right."

Yet Admiral Yamamoto was fated, like the sixteenth-century general's samurai, to "die sword in hand." For Japan's greatest warrior of World War II, that final moment came with shocking suddenness out of clear skies above the island of Bougainville in the Solomons on April 18, 1943.

During the preceding week, on a mild evening with the scent of spring in the air, I was on watch at the Communications Annex in Northwest Washington. Jim Hitchcock, who shared the watch with me that evening, came to me with the latest intercepted message; it had been fully broken out, and together we read it with astonishment and mounting excitement.

From: Commander, 8th Fleet

To: Commander, 1st Base Force
Commander, 11th Air Flotilla
Commander, 26th Air Flotilla
Commander, 958th Air Detachment
Chief, Ballale Defense Unit

The Commander-in-Chief Combined Fleet will inspect Ballale, Shortland, and Buin in accordance with the following:

1. 0600 depart Rabaul on board medium attack bomber (escorted by six fighters). 0800 arrive Ballale. Immediately depart for

Shortland on board subchaser (1st Base Force to prepare one boat), arriving at 0840. Depart Shortland 0945 by subchaser, arriving Ballale 1030. (For transportation prepare assault boat at Shortland and motor launch at Ballale.) 1100 depart Ballale by medium attack bomber arriving Buin 1110. Lunch at 1st Base Force Headquarters (Senior Staff Officer of Air Flotilla 26 to be present). 1400 depart Buin by medium attack bomber, arrive Rabaul 1540.

2. Inspection procedures: After being briefed on present status, the troops (patients at 1st Base Force Hospital) will be visited. There will be no interruptions, however, in the routine duties of the day.

3. Uniform will be the uniform of the day except that the commanding officers of the various units will be in combat dress with decorations.

4. In the event of inclement weather, there will be a postponement of one day.

The commander in chief of the Combined Fleet, Imperial Japanese Navy, was none other than Adm. Isoroku Yamamoto.

Both Hitchcock and I had no doubt about the importance of this message. The fate that placed the message in American hands well in advance of Yamamoto's trip offered one of those opportunities that were unlikely to come again. His plane, venturing into air space near positions seized by us on Guadalcanal and its vicinity, had to be intercepted at all costs and shot down. Yamamoto was far too dangerous an adversary and far too inspiring a leader to be spared so that he could endanger us, perhaps critically, at some future time.

Shooting down Yamamoto would be facilitated, we knew, by his insistence on punctuality. This was characteristic not only of the admiral but of the Japanese in general. In Japan the trains did not merely run on time; they could be checked with a stopwatch. The Tokyo-Osaka Express not only left Tokyo on the minute but arrived in Osaka, pulling into the station, as the sweep hand moved up to the minute.

"This is our chance to get rid of Yamamoto," Hitchcock said, giving me a meaningful glance.

"That's right. But can we send fighters that far?"

"I don't know. I just hope to hell we can."

Quite apart from his exalted position as commander in chief of the Combined Fleet, who was Yamamoto? As no other man he personified the modern Japanese Navy, which was largely his creation. Owing to his extraordinary dedication and drive as well as his visionary ideas about future naval strategy and tactics, which he advanced with the utmost tenacity, Japan developed its sea power to the point where, in 1941, it could more than cope with its leading rivals, the United States and Great Britain. Yamamoto tirelessly propounded the superiority of a navy built around air power in the form of carriers and a mix of level bombers, dive bombers, and torpedo planes that afforded maximum flexibility. As a result of his efforts the Imperial Navy surprised the world when it finally went into action.

This short and powerfully built, athletic, black-browed man with a razor-sharp intellect spanned in his person a period of nearly forty years between Togo's surprise attack on the Russian fleet at Port Arthur and his own spectacular surprise attack on the U.S. fleet at Pearl Harbor.

Yamamoto even possessed a physical memento of the famous Battle of Tsushima Strait in which Togo annihilated the main Russian battle fleet. As an ensign, Yamamoto had suffered injury in the engagement and lost two fingers of his left hand, ensuring that he would never forget the lessons of the Russo-Japanese War in waging the Second World War.

I felt a certain identification with Yamamoto, despite the difference in our ages, since I had followed him over the same ground many years later. Toward the end of World War I he spent two years as a graduate student in economics at Harvard. In the late twenties he served as Japanese naval attaché in Washington.

Yamamoto knew America well and liked Americans; moreover, he had a healthy respect for America's industrial strength and American ingenuity. While in the United States he traveled widely. He developed considerable proficiency in poker and bridge, reflecting his fondness for games in general.

His favorite game, however, was *go*, or Japanese chess, in which he was a formidable opponent. As a military man, he understood the principles of *go* better than most of his countrymen. *Go* is a deceptively simple game. The rules are easy to learn. The basic idea is to place your black or white counters on the board in such a way that you eventually completely surround your enemy's counters, thereby capturing them. But you have to take care at the same time to prevent your enemy from surrounding *you* in turn. Despite superficial appearances, the game is very subtle and requires even greater patience than the form of chess played in the West. And, as Yamamoto knew, it reflects an old samurai strategy based on deception, ruses, surprises, and ambushes.

Yamamoto showed in World War II that he had mastered these principles and could use them against the United States. At the same time, he never underrated the Americans. In this he shared the prevailing attitude of the Imperial Navy. Japanese naval officers were more widely traveled than their counterparts in the army; they possessed a more cosmopolitan outlook and, unlike most army officers, knew that their potential enemies across the seas might seem to be weak but were not to be despised.

It was the Japanese Army, from generals on down through the ranks, that enjoyed flexing its muscles and fanatically believed that it could overwhelm any foe. The Japanese Army could not visualize an enemy of equal strength, even after fighting an indecisive battle against Soviet troops on the Manchurian border; wherever it set down its collective boots, it swaggered along like a master, virtually unchallenged and unchallengeable.

The Japanese Army took over the government, installed its own man, General Tojo, as premier, and, over the objections of the Imperial Navy and Yamamoto personally, precipitated the country into war. Once he saw that war was inevitable, Yamamoto, as a patriot and a naval officer who had prepared all his life for war, decided to fight in a manner that would give Japan the best chance of winning. It was in this spirit that he resolved to carry out the surprise attack on Pearl Harbor.

After the crushing defeat at Midway, which had cost the Imperial Navy four big carriers, Yamamoto was disconsolate and locked himself in his cabin aboard the battleship *Yamato,* refusing to see all visitors. But he was too tough a fighter to remain inactive for long. The center of gravity had shifted to the southwest Pacific, where the Battle for Guadalcanal was in progress, and Yamamoto believed that the U.S. Navy could be forced to stand and fight; then the Imperial Navy, whose superiority he never doubted, could strike devastating blows at American heavy naval units and regain the initiative it had lost at Midway.

Yamamoto's hopes were not destined to be realized, despite the fact that he did succeed in engaging the U.S. fleet and inflicted severe damage on the enemy. Both sides suffered great losses in the naval war, but, unfortunately for the Japanese, American losses were easier to replace. The Americans lost the aircraft carriers *Wasp* and *Hornet,* five heavy cruisers, two light cruisers, and fourteen destroyers. Although the naval campaign ended in a virtual draw, the Japanese sustained their first great land defeat of the war at Guadalcanal, finally withdrawing their remaining forces from the island in February 1943. The failure to retake Guadalcanal from the Americans meant that all of the Solomons would fall sooner or later.

In an effort to inspire the Japanese forces with new spirit after the demoralizing defeat at Midway and the evacuation of Guadalcanal, Admiral Yamamoto went to Rabaul in New Britain in early April. At this point, he was directing a massive air offensive to destroy American air power and interdict Allied shipping in the Solomons and New Guinea. In his starched white uniform without medals, he conferred with khaki-clad top commanders on strategy for the next phase of the war. He also wished to inspect Japanese units in forward areas in order to familiarize himself at first hand with the situation. This was the reason for his short trip to the Bougainville area, but he could not have been unaware that the appearance of this revered war hero was bound to electrify the fighting men and boost their morale to new heights.

Yamamoto was so intense a competitor that he had banished even the thought of defeat from his mind, and whatever setbacks he encountered only made him all the more determined to win. Yet in some tiny corner of his being there must have taken root the seed of a suspicion that the tide was turning against Japan. He had never doubted that Japan could rampage through the Pacific for the first year or two, but he also recognized the danger that, failing to obtain decisive results within that time, Japan would face a fully mobilized America (*Beikoku*, the "Rice Country," as it was called!) capable of wearing down and eventually overwhelming Japan.

That was the principal reason why he had insisted on the surprise attack at Pearl Harbor—a treacherous attack in the eyes of Americans—and that was also the reason why he had struck at Midway in order to engage the U.S. fleet and win a decisive victory. His undertakings had failed, and now he recognized that it was only a matter of time before Japan would go down to defeat.

That night in Washington I walked outside the building in which I worked, through the grounds of the former girls' school, toward the snack bar in another small structure that stayed open all night. There was the promise of a clear day on the morrow, for the black arch of heaven bore a seemingly infinite number of starry jeweled lights. I smelled the cloying sweetness of honeysuckle in the woods that surrounded us.

As I strolled through the night, I could not help wondering about the fate of Admiral Yamamoto. Thousands of miles away from him, I was more aware of his imminent death than he could be.

It was not of course the function of officers on watch at the Naval Communications Annex to decide how decoded messages should be acted on. We had the task of breaking coded Japanese messages and translating them. Depending on their urgency, we saw to it that the substance of the messages was quickly transmitted through the chain of command. None of us had the authority even to suggest what sort of action, if any, should be taken on a message. *That* was up to Admiral King, chief of naval operations, and his commanders in the field.

Even so, it seemed to me that our fighter planes ought to be able to intercept the flight and shoot Yamamoto down. His death would undoubtedly have a profoundly distressing effect on the Japanese; they were sure to see it as an omen of disaster to come. While only a handful of leaders knew the truth about Midway, which the government had done its best to suppress, the loss of Guadalcanal was public knowledge and people in general must have already begun to suspect that the tide of the war had turned against Japan.

Yet the importance of killing Yamamoto did not end there. He was by far Japan's most able and imaginative military leader. No one else could replace him. As long as Yamamoto lived, we would never be able to rest easy, for he was the kind of man who instinctively recognized one's most vulnerable and unprotected spot and struck at it. Without him the spark would be gone from the Japanese high command.

I sat in the snack bar with a cup of coffee, thinking. At that hour of the night there were few people about. I kept wondering whether we would succeed in seizing this opportunity. At this distance it was impossible to tell what difficulties might lie in the way, but such an opportunity probably would not come again.

I did not know or even suspect that some of our own leaders would hesitate to pass the sentence of death on Yamamoto. I did not learn this until much later. Had I known at the time, I would have been both astonished and outraged.

Of course I understood the moral dilemma. If we considered it wrong to take a life, what could justify killing a man in war? Yet men were being killed all the time on both sides as a result of *our* actions. Our leaders ordered men into combat where they would kill and be killed. Killing seemed to be tolerable if the foe remained faceless and nameless. It was easier to kill by bombing from a high altitude than in hand-to-hand combat. Apparently the moral dilemma only became acute when you *knew* the man you were going to kill.

I looked across to another table where with obvious relish a fresh-faced yeoman was eating ham and eggs and a couple of pieces of toast. Maybe he was just out of high school; before long, no doubt, he would go to sea. Would he be one of those faceless ones on our side whose deaths would be mourned only by their families?

I admired Yamamoto. He was a foe who had earned my respect. In the course of a lifetime he had repeatedly demonstrated superb qualities of leadership in addition to strong character. He was a true patriot who loved his country and people, who had sought to avert war but now fought that war in a spirit of absolute selflessness and determination. How could you fail to esteem such a man?

Still, there was another side to the story. Admiral Yamamoto had planned and directed the attack that struck Pearl Harbor without warning, on a peaceful Sunday morning when most people had nothing more on their minds than to go to church or to spend the day sunbathing on the beach. Because of Yamamoto about twenty-four hundred Americans were killed that day. So Yamamoto was just as much our enemy as the airmen who dropped the bombs and the torpedoes, who strafed men on the ground.

There were few Americans who could feel very charitable toward Yamamoto, the man who had played a key role in precipitating us into an unwanted war. When Navy Secretary Frank Knox saw the intercepted message, however, he began to have some doubts about shooting down Yamamoto's plane. He asked the navy's judge advocate general for a ruling on the legality of assassination in such a case and discussed precedents for action of this kind. He took up the subject with a number of high-ranking officers and eventually with the president himself.

There was probably something to be said for examining the morality (not just the legality) of assassination in wartime, particularly when applied to political or civilian leaders. But military commanders? How did Yamamoto differ from any of the fighting men who served under him? How could we justify killing anonymous servicemen and civilians, including countless women and children, and at the same time draw the line at "assassinating" the commanders who waged war against us?

To spare Yamamoto in such circumstances might have suggested that there was a kind of unwritten conspiracy among the leaders on opposing sides to protect one another from the destruction and death meted out to the masses.

After World War I a vast reservoir of bitterness remained in the breasts of ordinary people on both sides who had observed that millions of men died in the mud of no-man's-land and on the barbed wire of the trenches while opposing generals sat in safety and comfort in villas and chateaus well behind the lines, playing their game of war. It would not have gone down well if, after *this* war, the people learned that enemy leaders had displayed such tender solicitude for one another in the midst of the general carnage.

Knox must have raised the problem with the president personally, and when orders were sent out to the south Pacific under Knox's signature, it was noted that President Roosevelt wanted top priority to be given to the mission of intercepting Yamamoto's plane and shooting it down. The message from Knox was routed to Admiral Halsey commanding the Third Fleet. Since the nearest base from which the American pilots could take off was on Guadalcanal, roughly four hundred miles from the point of interception, Halsey relayed the orders to Rear Adm. Marc Mitscher, Commander Air, Solomons, who had a mixed bag of navy, army, marine corps, and New Zealand pilots subordinate to him.

Mitscher decided that only the Army Air Corps P-38 Lightnings were capable of carrying out the mission. It seemed ironic that the P-38s should have come from Henderson Field. After all, Yamamoto was the man who had originally wanted to establish an airfield on Guadalcanal, and his efforts to build the air base had led to the Guadalcanal campaign. After the Japanese loss of the airfield, Yamamoto sent battleships and cruisers to try to put it out of operation; later he sent swarms of planes to batter Henderson

Field in order to prevent its use in an American counteroffensive. Now Yamamoto's own fate was to be decided by planes taking off from that same battered air base.

On the day before Yamamoto's flight Air Corps pilots Mitchell and Lanphier were summoned to headquarters, then located in a dugout. Their commanding officer showed them the top-secret message from Navy Secretary Knox ordering the mission. They returned to Mitchell's tent and started planning the whole operation. Mitchell had charts spread out on his cot and kept studying them throughout the evening.

Guadalcanal's nightly storm arrived, and rain descended in torrents while lightning flashed around the top of the mountains rising thousands of feet above the island. At the height of the storm some B-24s arrived from Port Moresby, carrying auxiliary tanks which the Lightnings needed in order to have enough fuel for their mission.

All through that wet night welders and fitters labored to equip the fighters with the auxiliary tanks while Mitchell, Lanphier, and the other pilots strove to get some sleep. When they arose at dawn, the weather was clear, bearing the promise of another hot tropical day, the sky like blue metal picking up some of the color of the darker sea. The pilots ate breakfast, feeling uneasy in their stomachs as they did before any mission whose outcome was far from certain.

On that Sunday, April 18, I was off duty and spent the day in Arlington, Virginia, visiting at the home of Charlotte, to whom I had become engaged in the meantime. I must have seemed preoccupied, and in fact I was, continuing to think about Yamamoto, wondering whether our fighters would succeed in intercepting his plane and shooting it down. My feelings were somewhat mixed, as I wanted to see him killed and yet I still half-regretted the death of such a gallant foe.

I found it hard to wait until Monday morning when I reported at the annex for my next watch. I saw the pleased faces of my fellow officers. "Mission accomplished," I heard someone say.

Then someone else told me: "They sent up sixteen fighters to intercept Yamamoto. It turned out that there were two bombers instead of one, so they shot down both planes."

The weather had been perfect, the sky a brilliant equatorial blue, the sea without whitecaps because there was almost no wind. Sixteen P-38s followed a circular course just above the waves, avoiding observation from Japanese-held islands like Munda, Rendova, and Shortland. The planes approached Bougainville from the west, where they would not be expected. At first the mountains of that island remained invisible. Then, at last, the planes floated up out of the haze at sea level and saw the mountains darkly outlined in the distance.

They could not wait long in the target area, or they would run out of fuel. Everything depended on the timing. If Yamamoto's flight was early or late, or if there had been any last-minute change in his route, the whole mission would be a failure. As it turned out, Yamamoto was at the exact time and place calculated from the decoded message. Almost immediately the Japanese formation, silvery shadows against the darker mountains, glided into view, apparently unaware of the close presence of the enemy.

The Japanese planes were only fifteen minutes away from their landing at Ballale when the Americans closed in. The two Mitsubishi bombers proved to be elusive prey, diving for the treetops of the jungle below. The sky filled with dogfights as the escorting Zeros sought to head off the intercepting fighters. Despite heroic efforts by the Japanese fighter pilots, some of the American fighters burst through to get the range of the bombers and blast away at them.

The American pilots had no way of knowing for certain which plane carried the illustrious passenger, and so it was vital to make sure that neither bomber escaped. They succeeded. Both bombers were shot down, one crashing in impenetrable jungle where dense black smoke boiled up, the other crash-landing in the sea where a few survivors could be rescued by Japanese patrol boats.

All but one of the American pilots returned from the mission, jubilantly reporting their success. Subsequent intercepted messages gave only indirect confirmation of Yamamoto's death. There were panicky exchanges of messages on circuits from Ballale and Rabaul to Truk and Tokyo. A search party had been organized at Ballale. Japanese planes and boats in the area showed extraordinary activity.

Finally, on May 21, 1943, a Japanese broadcast sorrowfully announced Admiral Yamamoto's death. That evening, if he had chosen to do so, Gabriel Heatter, the well-known commentator, could begin his own broadcast with the words, "Ah, there's bad news for Mr. Tojo in Tokyo tonight . . ."

President Roosevelt sent personal congratulations to Lanphier, presumed to be the pilot who shot down Yamamoto's plane. At the same time there was concern in Washington that any publicity could have harmful repercussions by giving away to the Japanese the fact that we had broken their codes.

General MacArthur, whose exploits throughout a long career marked him as one of the most gifted military leaders in modern times, had an ego to match his genius, and it was characteristic of him to claim the lion's share of the credit for Yamamoto's death. Although the record did not show that MacArthur had any personal involvement in the operation, he evidently felt that he was entitled to credit on at least two counts: Halsey, as he said, had been placed under his "strategic command for the Solomons campaign," and the pilots who actually shot Yamamoto down belonged to the Army Air Corps.

MacArthur wrote in his *Reminiscences:* "On April 18th we made one of the most significant strikes of the war. Our Air Force shot down the commander-in-chief of the Japanese Combined Fleet, Admiral Isoroku Yamamoto. . . ." Not content with this general assertion of his involvement, MacArthur referred to the intercepted message and went on to say: "There was much skepticism that the message was a hoax, but *I* [my italics] knew Yamamoto as a front-line fighter who always pressed forward to the decisive points of contact. Major John W. Mitchell, commander of the 339th Fighter Squadron, was detailed to take his fighter unit and intercept at the rendezvous point. . . ."

It was with genuine regret that MacArthur accepted the ban on publicity: "Washington lauded the action as one of the most important bags of the war, but labeled it top secret and forbade its publication, fearing it would jeopardize the work of the cryptanalytic division. And Lanphier became the unsung hero of an extraordinary exploit."

Admiral Yamamoto's remains were cremated at Bougainville, and the ashes, in a little pine box, were flown to Truk for a memorial ceremony aboard his flagship *Musashi*. The same ship transported the ashes to Japan when a large force of Yamamoto's beloved Combined Fleet, commanded by Adm. Mineichi Koga, who had been named as his successor, sailed from Truk on May 16 bound for Tokyo. GZ had earlier become aware of this ship movement, which came in response to the invasion of the western Aleutians by U.S. forces.

On June 5, 1943, Yamamoto received a state funeral in Tokyo. In the presence of dense crowds silently mourning the fallen hero, a solemn funeral procession wound its way from Hibiya Park in downtown Tokyo, near the Imperial Palace, to the cemetery where part of the ashes were interred in an urn next to Admiral Togo. The state funeral took place on the anniversary of Togo's own funeral, thereby once again linking the careers of Japan's greatest naval heroes.

On that same day, completely unaware of Yamamoto's state funeral, I married Charlotte in Arlington, Virginia. We had received a letter from Sy Millstein with the Amphibious Force in the southwest Pacific:

> Dear Charlotte and Ed: I can honestly say that I was made as happy by the good news as if it had been my own heart involved. Ed's letter was so beautiful in its pure joy that I just had to sit there and read it over and over, and relive the whole thing from the time Ed came home and told me he had met such a sweet girl and from

14. Charlotte Whelan Van Der Rhoer in 1943.

then on never stopped pouring his feelings out. I remember each up and down in the affair—as judged by Ed's spirits after a date. I remember the terrific redness of Ed's face as he returned from a phone conversation with you and I envied him like hell the pure sweet feeling of love he had for you. I envy you both now yet I am happy with you and hope that some day we can all be happy together again. To hell with congratulations—I just think it's wonderful and tomorrow I shall be the drunkest Yank in Australia—in your honor. . . .

We spent our honeymoon in the pleasant if unpretentious little town of Luray, Virginia, near the Blue Ridge Mountains. During that week, thousands of mourners came to Yamamoto's hometown of Nagaoka and filed past the urn containing his remaining ashes. The urn stood next to his uniform and sword. At a second funeral these ashes were placed next to those of his schoolteacher father in a Buddhist temple. The stone that marked his grave was, at his request, one inch smaller than that of his father.

In years to come, a statue of Yamamoto would be erected at the Kasumigaura flying school, which he had once commanded, but the statue had to be removed when MacArthur, seeking to eradicate Japanese militarism, ordered the destruction of military statues at the time of the American occupation. The statue was thrown into a lake, but part of it—Yamamoto's head and shoulders—would eventually be retrieved and restored to a place in a small park in the center of Nagaoka beside a replica of the typical house, made of wood with straw mats and sliding rice-paper doors, in which Yamamoto had been born. His original birthplace had met with destruction during one of the last American firebomb raids on Japan.

Most Americans would remember only that Yamamoto perished in his downed plane at Bougainville.

Just as Gen. Stonewall Jackson's death at Chancellorsville was fatal to the Confederate cause in the American Civil War, Admiral Yamamoto's death was fatal to Japan's cause in World War II.

The War of the Marus

AS it took shape in the early months of the war, the Greater East Asia Coprosperity Sphere represented the realization of the dreams of Japanese expansionists.

Japan, a highly industrialized nation, lacked essential raw materials. To the coal and iron of Manchuria seized in the thirties there now came the rubber and tin of Malaya, the rice of Indochina, the oil of the Dutch East Indies. Raw materials could be transported to Japan, processed into finished goods, and reshipped to the principal consumers, who in this period became the armed forces on the continent of Asia and scattered throughout the islands of the Pacific.

Japan's merchant marine appeared to be more than adequate for this important task, since at the start of the war it consisted of over six million tons to which there were continual additions through new construction, salvage, or capture.

At first one of the main patterns of shipping followed the flow of raw materials from the south to the Japanese home islands and then back again in the form of manufactured goods for the armed forces in southern areas. However, after the conquest of Southeast Asia and adjoining offshore islands of the Pacific had been completed, the pattern changed. Now merchant ships carried raw materials from the south to Japan, but on the return trip the ships went out in ballast or only partly loaded. Another route was from Japan to the central Pacific islands, carrying military supplies, but the ships on this route returned to Japan empty.

American critics have pointed out that Japanese shipping could have been more fully utilized by developing a triangular routing: transport of natural resources from Southeast Asia to Japan, military goods from Japan to the Pacific islands, and travel in ballast from those islands to Southeast Asia. Instead of remaining empty one-half of the time, the Japanese merchant marine would have then been unused only one-third of the time.

The United States could not prevent Japan from gaining control of natural resources in the south, but it could do the next best thing by attacking the merchant shipping that had to transport raw materials back to Japan and the finished goods to outlying regions.

In this connection, a curious disparity in policy between the U.S. and Japanese navies came to light. Immediately after Pearl Harbor the U.S. chief of naval operations ordered unrestricted submarine warfare against the Japanese empire, recognizing that the latter's merchant shipping offered a vulnerable spot that had to be attacked at all costs. On the other hand, Japanese submariners shared the disdain of their fellow navy men for targets other than warships. Ignoring Allied shipping, they concentrated on missions in support of fleet operations. Thus they apparently learned nothing from the experience of U-boats in World War I or the Battle of the Atlantic in World War II. Even their German allies failed to shake their conviction that Japanese submarines should not be risked against lesser targets than warships.

While Japanese submariners continued to disdain the role of commerce raiders, American submariners were hampered in their operations by technical problems. The biggest problem came from defective torpedoes that ran at a depth lower than they were set for, often passing completely under the ships at which they were aimed, or exploded prematurely, or even turned out to be duds. The submarine *Tinosa* plumbed the depths of frustration in July 1943, when she fired no fewer than nine torpedoes and obtained nine solid hits on a large Japanese tanker, yet not one of the nine torpedoes exploded. After this unhappy experience had been reported, the Bureau of Ordnance finally recognized the need to do something about the torpedoes, and the situation gradually improved.

American misadventures with the torpedo belied our vaunted technical know-how, but should have properly been blamed on the penny-wise and pound-foolish philosophy underlying prewar naval budgeting which made it too expensive to fire live torpedoes in practice. If we had tested live torpedoes in peacetime exercises, we would not have had to learn our mistakes under wartime conditions when we inevitably lost valuable time and precious opportunities.

Meanwhile the Japanese had developed a magnificent torpedo, the 24-inch Long Lance, which could carry a thousand pounds of explosives eleven miles at forty-nine knots or twenty miles at thirty-six knots. Not only was it more dependable, but it also had greater speed, longer range, and a more powerful charge than its American counterpart.

Nevertheless, the Imperial Navy neglected the chance to blunt any Allied offensive in the Pacific by using submarines as commerce raiders, and its mistaken appreciation of the role of merchant shipping in wartime extended to a failure to develop any plan for convoying Japanese ships. In the early months of the war these ships were independently routed. When I first arrived in Washington in the spring of 1942, the Japanese instituted a limited convoy system. Up to the time of the Battle of the Coral Sea, however, our submarines had sunk only about thirty-five merchant ships. Between Midway and the invasion of Guadalcanal we succeeded in sinking about sixty thousand tons of shipping, and in July 1942, reacting to growing losses, the Japanese established the First Convoy Escort Fleet with headquarters on Taiwan.

Yet Japan never gave due weight to convoys, which the offense-minded Imperial Navy deemed unworthy of protection. Warships, in the Japanese view, were to be used against other warships. On the basis of such doctrine the Combined Fleet refused to allow its destroyers to perform convoy duty even when they could have done so without hindering their normal operations. It did not seem to have occurred to Japanese naval leaders that enemy submarines attacking convoys could also be classified as warships.

The heavy toll of Japanese shipping was due not only to the increasing skill of U.S. submarines and their constant technical improvement. Communications intelligence again played a large part in the damage we were inflicting. American submarines had no need to go in search of enemy ships, nor did they have to waste long days and hours lying in wait for prey along shipping lanes. Armed with communications intelligence, they knew exactly where to go and what they could expect to find when they got there. As a result, our submarines became steadily more deadly.

The most important aspect of this information was its use in reporting noon positions of convoys, which became known for a number of days in advance, usually corresponding to the length of the whole trip. This meant of course that we had ample time to alert our submarines and send them to the correct points in order to intercept those convoys. When messages giving noon positions were decoded, our colleagues at FRUPAC (Fleet Radio Unit, Pacific), the Pearl Harbor branch of communications intelligence, transmitted them by direct line to ComSubPac, whose operations officer radioed the detailed information to submarines patrolling those areas. Considering the vastness of the Pacific, the ability to go straight to the target, do the job, and get out meant an enormous saving in the wear and tear of submarine duty. The establishment of an advanced submarine base on Midway Island saved our submarines twenty-four hundred miles of travel, which they formerly covered to and from Pearl Harbor (rather than Midway), but the average patrol still did not last much more than a month, and submarines had been able in some cases to spend no more than five days in their assigned areas. Thus the effectiveness of the submarines in destroying enemy shipping benefited tremendously from detailed information.

Apart from the knowledge concerning the location of convoys, communications intelligence also gave precise data on the composition of those convoys and their escort vessels as well as the nature of the cargoes. As the war went on, ComSubPac became more selective in assigning targets to his submarines as a means of striking at Japan's greatest vulnerabilities and crippling its war economy.

For obvious reasons, the American submarines encountered varying degrees of difficulty in observing the results of their attacks. Occasionally they could remain near the surface long enough to confirm the sinking of a ship, but in many cases a submarine's torpedo attack met with an immediate reaction in the form of a depth charge counterattack by escort vessels, and the submarine was forced to dive without an instant's delay in order to survive. At times the submarine claimed to have sunk a ship when in fact the ship had only been damaged. Moreover, the submarine was seldom in a position to identify the victim in other than general terms.

Communications intelligence came to the assistance of the submarine force in yet another way. It provided information on the results of submarine attacks based on Japanese contact reports— sometimes even giving the submarine a second chance to return and finish off a ship that was dead in the water but still afloat after the ship supposedly had been sunk. And finally it gave a positive identification of the submarine's victim.

Hundreds of messages giving the noon positions of Japanese convoys or independently routed ships were intercepted and broken and the information relayed via ComSubPac to submarines on patrol. The messages were highly standardized. A typical message could run as follows:

CONVOY A22 (HITACHI MARU, NO. 1 HAINAN MARU, TOYOKUNI MARU, AKASHI MARU, TSURUGA MARU, JUHO MARU, NANIWA MARU) ESCORTED BY AKIKAZE. PORT

15. Periscope photo taken aboard the U.S. submarine *Wahoo*, March 21, 1943, showing the Japanese *Nittsu Maru* sinking after a torpedo attack in the Yellow Sea. *National Archives.*

OF ORIGIN, OSAKA: DESTINATION, MANILA. ESTIMATED NOON POSITIONS: NOVEMBER 11, 32-10 N 134-43 E; NOVEMBER 12, 29-15 N 130-45 E; NOVEMBER 13, 26-25 N 123-30 E; NOVEMBER 14, 22-40 N 119-35 E; NOVEMBER 15, 17-25 N 119-15 E. ESTIMATED TIME OF ARRIVAL MANILA NOVEMBER 15 2300 HOURS.

After information of this type had been transmitted to our submarines, Japanese contact reports would reveal subsequent developments. I might receive, for example, a contact report concerning a submarine attack on November 14:

TODAY AT 2:45 P.M. _____ _____ MARU RECEIVED AN

ATTACK BY AN ENEMY SUBMARINE AND WAS HIT BY
TWO TORPEDOES. SHE EXPLODED AND SANK IMMEDI-
ATELY. POSITION: 21 DEGREES 50 MINUTES NORTH LAT-
ITUDE, _____ DEGREES 5 MINUTES EAST LONGITUDE.
WE ARE RESCUING SURVIVORS. REQUEST AIR COVER.

The three blanks in the message represented unrecovered information that I tried to deduce. The name of the ship was particularly important for the navy's order-of-battle on the enemy, and the
exact position of the attack would be helpful in matching up the
message with the submarine's own report.

In such a case, I checked first of all with the people in the
middle room next to mine and learned that in the light of the message we had received earlier the ship in question had probably
belonged to the A22 convoy. Using the noon positions, I fixed the
east longitude on November 14 at 119 degrees, thereby making a
tentative recovery of one of the missing code groups.

Then I carefully examined the names of the ships listed in the
message concerning the A22 convoy and, after further research, by
both eliminating and narrowing down possibilities, I succeeded in a
probable identification of the sunken ship as the *Akashi Maru* out
of Kobe, seventy-five hundred gross tons according to our naval
records.

Thus communications intelligence sources combined to help
the submarines in their steadily more effective campaign of attri-
tion against the Japanese merchant marine.

For a long time the Japanese continued to use a limited convoy
system even after it became apparent that their losses were becoming serious. Small convoys with a single escort vessel were easy
prey for a submarine, which simply attacked at the point farthest
removed from the escort vessel. The results were still more satisfy-
ing from the American point of view when a couple of submarines
made a coordinated attack—after the first submarine attacked, the
escort vessel would dash to that end of the convoy and the second
submarine could carry out an attack at leisure on the other end.
Yet the Japanese high command was reluctant to institute large

16. Periscope photo taken aboard the U.S. submarine *Puffer*, showing a torpedo exploding alongside the Japanese *Teiko Maru*, sunk February 22, 1944.

convoys with many well-armed escort vessels despite experience that indicated that this was by far the most effective technique.

During the early stages of the war in the Atlantic, U-boats inflicted catastrophic merchant marine losses on the British, bringing them to the brink of starvation. Gradually, however, the British evolved methods for protecting ships in large convoys, perfecting antisubmarine techniques that turned the tables and subjected the U-boats themselves to such heavy losses that it became nearly suicidal for the U-boats to undertake attacks. In this the British received great aid from the Americans, and both pooled their resources in communications intelligence to locate and destroy U-boats.

The Japanese objection to large convoys, as in so many other things, was doctrinal. It stemmed from a belief that convoy duty was purely defensive, and since both the Japanese Army and Navy emphasized offense and scorned defense, it took some time for this error in judgment to be recognized. Their conviction that "the best defense is a good offense," well rooted in American sports such as football, had its adherents on our side. Nevertheless, from the point of view of the U.S. Navy, there was no real contradiction here, because convoy duty had both defensive and offensive purposes.

While the Japanese regarded it as a waste of good warships to assign them to convoys, the U.S. Navy sought not only to protect merchant ships but also to look upon convoys as bait for enemy submarines. This would enable the escort vessels to engage in antisubmarine warfare and annihilate them.

It did not happen to be effective as a means of destroying *Japanese* submarines simply because, as we have seen, the Imperial Navy failed to employ its submarines as commerce raiders. By this neglect, the Japanese forfeited the opportunity to weaken the enemy still further when he was weakest and to blunt any hoped-for American counteroffensive in the Pacific.

By preference, the Japanese submarines took part in offensive naval operations and attacked the most difficult targets, enemy warships, which inevitably led to powerful counterattacks and heavy losses on their side. The success of these submarines in sinking enemy warships was not important enough to offset their failures.

In later stages of the war their missions became far more defensive than they would have been if they had assumed the despised part of commerce raiders, since they were used increasingly in resupply operations on behalf of island garrisons isolated and cut off by American island hopping across the Pacific. Submarines being ill-suited to such operations, they suffered heavy losses in a defense-oriented and passive role.

As their merchant ship losses continued to grow, the Japanese belatedly realized that the convoy system had to be changed. In November 1943 they created a Grand Escort Command Headquarters that set up larger convoys with a number of escort vessels.

American submarines struck back with wolf-pack tactics and, in spite of increased losses, continued to inflict heavy damage, particularly as a result of their knowing the convoy's noon positions. They successfully employed various techniques, one of them being to lie in wait at the noon positions and fire a spread of torpedoes at the convoys as they approached.

In the following year the Grand Escort Command Headquarters was subordinated directly to the Combined Fleet. This step might have been motivated by the hope that the convoy system would receive more effective support from the Combined Fleet. In reality, nothing could stop the decline of the Japanese merchant marine, and as the decline continued and even accelerated, Japan encountered massive difficulties in maintaining its war machine.

One of ComSubPac's special targets, based on Japanese vulnerabilities, was tankers carrying vital fuel supplies from the East Indies. By war's end our submarines had sunk an estimated 110 oil-carrying ships, causing a fuel shortage that afflicted the empire with a form of creeping paralysis.

Because of the lack of aviation fuel, Japan could not train enough pilots to replace the losses in flight personnel sustained with increasing severity from the time of Midway onward. Because of this, during the last large fleet engagement of the war, the Battle for Leyte Gulf, Japanese aircraft carriers were virtually without aircraft to throw into the battle, owing to the shortage of trained pilots, and could only be used as decoys in an effort to draw U.S. fleet units away from the main scene of struggle.

Still earlier, fuel shortages had already forced the Imperial Navy to divide its forces, sending heavy surface ships south to operate near fuel supplies—some of which they used in dangerously volatile form, unrefined, directly from the well!— while aircraft carriers remained in home waters where they could undergo repair and their pilots could be trained. This division made it extremely difficult, if not impossible, for the Combined

Fleet to coordinate its efforts at a critical moment in the Battle for Leyte Gulf. The ensuing defeat marked the end of the Imperial Navy as an effective fighting force.

Although Japanese tankers constituted special targets for our submarines, communications intelligence sometimes singled out other special targets of opportunity.

Shortly after U.S. troops invaded Attu in the Aleutians, which had been captured by the Japanese at the time of the Battle of Midway, GZ received information that Admiral Koga, the new commander in chief of the Combined Fleet, had departed from Truk on May 16, 1943, with a considerable force of ships, bound for Tokyo Bay. Apart from his flagship *Musashi*, other fleet units accompanying him were the battleships *Haruna* and *Kongo*, the carrier *Hiyo*, the cruisers *Tone* and *Chikuma*, and five destroyers.

Clearly the Japanese high command was weighing the advisability of a counterattack against the U.S. north Pacific force. Admiral Koga, however, was also worried about reports of American offensive preparations at Pearl Harbor and in the Solomons–New Guinea area. Given these preoccupations, the commander in chief of the Combined Fleet hesitated with a northern move and finally took the easy course of doing nothing.

In view of the concentration of the Combined Fleet near Tokyo, ComSubPac ordered the submarine *Trigger* to a patrol area off Tokyo Bay, where she remained during the time Admiral Yamamoto, Koga's predecessor, was receiving a state funeral in Tokyo. On June 10, when she was about to give up the long vigil and return to Pearl Harbor, *Trigger* spotted the carrier *Hiyo* with an escort of two destroyers sortieing from Tokyo Bay. *Trigger* succeeded in getting two torpedo hits on the big carrier (two others were believed to have exploded prematurely), and *Hiyo* suffered the ignominy of being towed into Yokosuka by the cruiser *Isuzu*. She did not return to action for many months. When she finally did, she was the only combat ship to be sunk in the first Battle of the Philippine Sea in June 1944 (although two other Japanese carriers were sunk by U.S. submarines in the preliminaries of that battle).

THE WAR OF THE MARUS

The skill, daring, and brilliant accomplishments of American submariners in the Pacific war cannot be praised too highly. Nonetheless, they were greatly assisted in their exploits by communications intelligence, which supplied them with vital information directing them to their targets. Out of a total of eight million tons of Japanese shipping destroyed during the war, no less than five million tons were accounted for by the U.S. submarine force.

CHAPTER 8

Island Hopping: Grim Military Hopscotch

UNDER Rosey Mason the people of GZ had come a long way. They had accompanied Admirals Takeo Takagi and Chuichi Hara in the Battle of the Coral Sea; Admiral Yamamoto, commander in chief of the Combined Fleet, as he hatched his plans for the Battle of Midway; Admiral Nagumo at Midway Island when he lost four big carriers and his nerve along with them; and Yamamoto again as he maneuvered his Main Force to seek a decision in the same battle, only to be forced to withdraw and acknowledge defeat. During the Guadalcanal campaign we closely followed the deliberations and decisions of the Imperial Navy General Staff as well as the surface operations conducted by admirals such as Mikawa and Tanaka, who performed brilliantly but vainly until the Japanese were forced to withdraw once more.

When the U.S. Joint Chiefs of Staff issued orders for an offensive in the central Pacific, first of all against the outer ramparts of the Japanese empire in the Gilberts and the Marshalls, the American commanders were not thinking of island hopping along the lines that developed in the course of time. They viewed the strategy only as a gradual, phased campaign to penetrate into the Japanese stronghold by seizing one island chain after the other, conquering all the islands in one group before moving on to the next group. The idea of bypassing some of the most powerful enemy bases only emerged later in the face of the practical difficulties that we encountered.

Before the war the Japanese had dropped an iron curtain of secrecy over their island possessions in Micronesia such as the Marianas, Carolines, and Marshalls. By barring access to this area they concealed from prying eyes their construction of military bases and other preparations for war—activities that, then and later, purported to be solely for "cultural" purposes.

When war began, the United States possessed remarkably little information about what was going in those islands. After they captured the neighboring Gilberts, which had been under British rule, the Japanese proceeded to seal off this archipelago too, accelerating the process as a result of a raid on Makin by U.S. Marines that aroused doubt about the reliability of the local population.

The code breaking in which GZ was engaged enabled the navy to possess intelligence on the whole area that could be obtained in no other way. The garrisons in the Marshalls and Gilberts regularly reported their strength in messages breaking down the figures into combat effective, sick, and wounded. Available stores, including ammunition, were also reported on a monthly or weekly basis, depending on the situation. The islands that had airfields reported on the number of planes that were fully operational, partly operational, and out of order, as well as the up-to-date fuel supply. From all these messages directed to higher headquarters we could obtain an overall view of the situation in the principal islands.

At the same time we learned about the movements of marus carrying supplies and reinforcements to the island as well as the movements of aircraft, including regular patrols and exercises.

In September 1943, when a U.S. task force that included a fast carrier, the new *Lexington,* and the light carriers *Princeton* and

Belleau Wood launched strikes at Makin and Tarawa in the Gilberts, I could extract a considerable amount of information about the results of those raids. Caught by surprise, both Makin and Tarawa suffered very heavy losses in personnel. Tarawa's airfield on Betio Island was temporarily put out of action, with eight out of sixteen planes destroyed. The carrier planes also sank a maru in the lagoon along with three picket boats (during the invasion of Tarawa Japanese swam out to the wreckage of the freighter and used it as cover to attack marines in the landing force).

In November 1943, when other carrier strikes at Tarawa took place just before the invasion, we found out that the forces on Betio Island had expended most of their ammunition during the raids, making them that much more vulnerable to the amphibious operation that was about to begin.

As early as the middle of 1943 it took no great surge of imagination to discern the two-pincered Allied strategy: one pincer moving up through New Guinea and the Bismarcks, the other directly westward through the central Pacific, with both pincers meeting to crack the nut represented by the Philippines or, possibly, Taiwan. If successful, the powerful forces that joined at this point would strike north together past Okinawa to the main islands of Japan.

Although it could foresee the threat of such an offensive, the Imperial Navy could do little to prevent a drive through the central Pacific. The cumulative losses suffered in the period since Midway had drastically sapped the strength of the Japanese fleet, both on the surface and in the air.

Admiral Koga took the Combined Fleet to the Marshalls on at least two occasions without encountering the enemy. Meanwhile the U.S. Pacific Fleet had not only replaced its losses but also had achieved both a quantitative and qualitative leap in strength. When in November 1943 the United States finally struck at the Gilberts, the Combined Fleet made no effort to interfere, failing to engage the American covering force that was awaiting just such a move.

The U.S. Army troops that landed at Makin had little trouble in subduing the enemy, for, as we knew in GZ, the main island of

Butaritari was defended by only about eight hundred Japanese servicemen of various types, including some Special Naval Landing Force troops commanded by a lieutenant, junior grade.

Tarawa, however, proved to be another story. U.S. ships forced an entrance into the lagoon so that the marines could land from the lagoon side where defenses were considered weaker. American lack of experience in amphibious operations and the die-hard resistance of the garrison, protected not only by strong fortifications but also by primitive yet effective layers of coconut logs and coral sand, exacted a heavy toll of the attackers. The Japanese defenders fought almost to the last man, only one officer and sixteen enlisted men surrendering out of some three thousand men (apart from a hundred Korean laborers). U.S. losses included one thousand men killed out of a total attacking force of eighteen thousand men.

In GZ it was business as usual while we followed the course of the struggle with acute concern, intercepting the first of a type of message that we would see many times in the capture of Pacific islands from the Japanese.

The last message sent out by the Japanese garrison on Tarawa early on November 22 said: "Our weapons have been destroyed and now everyone will attempt a final charge. May His Majesty the Emperor live ten thousand years!"

At this time I was living in McLean Gardens, an apartment development located just off Wisconsin Avenue on the former site of Mrs. Evelyn Walsh McLean's Friendship estate. The development had been finished in the first part of 1943, and my wife and I moved into the apartment right after our marriage. We were directly opposite a temporary building housing the General Accounting Office, and when I had to sleep during the day I kept waking up at the sound of bells that seemed to regulate all the activities across the street.

The Naval Communications Annex was separated from McLean Gardens by a stretch of dense woods, and since many people assigned to the annex lived in McLean Gardens, the navy had built a

17. Marines move out from the beachhead at Tarawa, November 1943, into the smoke-covered Japanese airstrip.

path up a steep slope through the woods to the back gate of the annex.

When I was on the evening or mid watches, I carried an electric lantern to light my way through the dark woods, which had no illumination except at the gate and from the streets in McLean Gardens which approached the end of the path on that side. In the spring the woods carried the heavy perfumed scent of honeysuckle; in summer it was a repository of coolness trapped against the heat of the day; and in autumn the air had a snap, and one's feet brushed through piles of fallen red and gold and brown leaves.

Between the annex and McLean Gardens I made the uneasy

transition from the war to the deceptive peace that surrounded us in Washington. Those of us who were in the same situation knew that the real issues of war and peace were being fought far away in the vast, seemingly limitless, spaces of the Pacific, the stormy Atlantic, and war-torn Europe and Africa. How long the peace here would last depended on what happened there.

In the annex the war with Japan was strictly compartmentalized from the war with Germany for obvious security reasons. GZ's occasionally overlapping interests were handled through Comdr. Knight McMahon, who represented the German side of the war, where significant results were being achieved against the German U-boats through communications intelligence, not to speak of the even greater achievements in penetrating into Nazi Germany's top secrets through the ENIGMA machine. McMahon, who was a gentleman to the core as well as a man of genuine intellect, often proved to be of invaluable assistance in coordinating our mutual interests.

Our successes had also created difficulties to some extent in the form of bottlenecks. A much more serious cause of congestion might have been the machine room, where all the mechanical runs on which we relied were processed. Thanks to Comdr. Bob Sage, who was the boss of the machine room, we seldom had cause to complain.

When I saw the blond, personable Bob Sage on his way through our room, I invariably stopped him and said, "Bob, what about those new runs I'm waiting for?"

Sage was an unflappable type. "You'll have them this afternoon," he said, unruffled. He never failed to keep his promise.

After the American invasion of Makin, Tarawa, and other islands in the Gilberts, most of us saw in the Imperial Navy's failure to intervene a confession of weakness, an admission that the Japanese fleet was no more prepared to oppose an invasion of the Marshalls to the north than in the Gilberts. American commanders immediately set about planning for an early seizure of the Marshalls. There was, however, a difference of opinion between Admiral Nimitz and his immediate subordinates. Admirals Spruance and Richmond K. Turner favored the capture of the outer islands of Maloelap and Wotje as a first step, but Nimitz decided to assault Kwajalein, the heart of the archipelago, while bypassing the other islands.

Nimitz's decision surprised not only his own commanders but also the Japanese high command. The enemy leaders also assumed that the United States would first attack the outer atolls and so gave top priority to defense supplies and manpower allocated to Maloelap and Wotje and also Mili and Jaluit. Their counter-measures were clearly reflected in intercepted messages. Meanwhile, it was apparent that Kwajalein continued to be relatively lightly defended. This was not so much a matter of troop strength as of fortifications, which were less formidable than those encountered by the Second Marine Division at Tarawa.

The extent to which these decoded messages influenced Nimitz in reaching his decision remained unknown to us. Nevertheless, it came as no surprise when the assault on Kwajalein began at the very end of January 1944. The American commanders had learned from the mistakes made at Tarawa, such as inadequate preliminary bombardment, mixups in landing maneuvers, and lack of heavy weapons ashore in direct support of the troops. As a result the Kwajalein attack went off much more smoothly.

By the time the coral atoll of Kwajalein had been secured, the Americans were already aiming at a new objective: Eniwetok in the western Marshalls, an important staging point for planes taking off from Truk and Saipan. Nimitz gave a prompt go-ahead for this operation and the landings at Eniwetok took place within a short time after those at Kwajalein, in the second half of February 1944.

We in GZ were watching the Combined Fleet for signs that Admiral Koga planned to sortie and oppose our next moves in the Marshalls. We did not know that Koga had dispersed his carrier air groups to defend Rabaul and hence was in no position to undertake any action. Moreover, unknown to us at the time, the Japanese high command had virtually written off the Gilberts and the Marshalls and decided to maintain a new defense line based on the Marianas, the Carolines, western New Guinea, and Timor.

Although we possessed rather accurate information about the strength of the Eniwetok garrison, thanks to the breaking of coded messages, we did not have details concerning the dispositions of the First Amphibious Brigade of the Japanese Army, which had arrived there only a month before our invasion, on the various islands of the atoll.

Both air and submarine reconnaissance failed to disclose the presence of enemy troops on the southern islands of Parry and Eniwetok despite the fact that the two islands were strongly defended. Parry and Eniwetok happened to be largely deserted coconut plantations where dense tropical foliage under the palm trees remained impenetrable to aerial photography.

When our amphibious elements forced an entrance into the Eniwetok lagoon, the Japanese commander ordered his men to lie low and avoid disclosing their presence. Fortunately we had made our first objective Engebi Island in the north, where there was an airfield. Among papers captured on that island an intelligence group found information revealing that the Japanese had considerable troop strength on the two southern islands. As a result, the U.S. commander changed the plan of campaign, and the islands were seized one at a time against fierce resistance on the part of an enemy that was well dug in. We took only sixty-four prisoners out of a garrison estimated at thirty-five hundred men because the Japanese preferred to fight to the death or commit suicide rather than surrender.

Life at the Communications Annex went on its way, seemingly unaffected by the fortunes of war. As usual, Mason was the first one on duty every morning before the mid watch went off duty, despite the fact that he drove in all the way from Manassas, Virginia, thirty miles away, over roads which at that time could not be considered superhighways by any stretch of the imagination. He liked to take time off in the late morning or early afternoon to play tennis on one of the courts that we had inherited from the girls' school. He worried that his health (supposedly he suffered from ulcers) could prematurely end his naval career. And he kept hoping for a sea command in order to qualify for an eventual promotion beyond the rank of captain. In the meantime, he did not relax his grip on GZ, continuing to keep the pressure on us.

In June 1944 the attention of the world was focused on the Allied invasion of Europe, but in the same month the United States struck at Saipan and the southern Marianas, one of the anchors of the new Japanese defense line. As a prelude to the invasion of Saipan, Admiral Mitscher's Task Force 58 had flung its planes at Truk, compelling the Combined Fleet to retreat farther westward to Palau and neutralizing Truk to the point where its usefulness as a naval and air base was reduced almost to zero. Next Iwo Jima and Chichi Jima came under attack from our carrier forces in order to prevent air reinforcements from Japan from reaching Saipan.

The decision of the Joint Chiefs of Staff to invade Saipan and the southern Marianas stemmed directly from their decision to bypass rather than attempt to seize Truk, regarded by some military leaders as the "Gibraltar of the Pacific" or the "Japanese Pearl Harbor." Truk had been the Imperial Navy's most valuable base during the first two years of the war. Bypassing Truk was a wise move, since the atoll was in reality a drowned mountain range and afforded very strong if not impregnable defensive positions. Besides, it had already been proven that Truk could be neutralized by naval air power so that its capture did not appear to be worth the expensive price in lives and materiel we would be forced to pay.

Thus Saipan, which would bring Japan itself within the range of U.S. land-based bombers, was the obvious next target. An amphibious force carrying nearly 130,000 marines and soldiers, the largest force yet thrown into the cross-Pacific drive, set out for our objectives in the Marianas. Considering that Saipan was only 1,350 miles from Japan and belonged to the vital Japanese defense line, we could expect a violent reaction from the Imperial Navy.

In GZ we carefully and attentively watched the movements of

important naval units. After the Combined Fleet retreated from Truk, we discovered that a new force, the First Mobile Fleet, had been established with its base at Tawitawi, a tiny island off the northeastern tip of Borneo, close to the island of Mindanao in the Philippines. This had been one of the first steps taken by Adm. Soemu Toyoda, who succeeded the late Admiral Koga as commander in chief of the Combined Fleet, after receiving instructions from the Naval General Staff to put an end to his predecessor's passive policy and prepare to carry the attack to the enemy. (Admiral Koga was killed when his plane bound for the Philippines on March 31 was lost in a storm.)

There could have been no greater acknowledgment of the effectiveness of Admiral Mitscher's Task Force 58 than Toyoda's obvious imitation of this force in creating the First Mobile Fleet, built around carriers, and placing it under the command of Vice-Adm. Jisaburo Ozawa, Japan's foremost naval air officer.

Despite its central location, Tawitawi proved to be an unfortunate choice for a base. As soon as our communications intelligence identified the new base of the Mobile Fleet, U.S. submarines converged on that area and guarded all the outlets to the sea.

As expected, the invasion of Saipan triggered Japanese retaliation and led directly to the Battle of the Philippine Sea. Admiral Toyoda sent the First Mobile Fleet, strengthened by the super-battleships *Musashi* and *Yamato* and a force of cruisers and destroyers, to give battle to the U.S. Fifth Fleet in the southern Marianas.

Apart from communications intelligence, our submarines were in a position to observe the sortie of the First Mobile Fleet and follow its progress toward the prospective battle area. U.S. forces had landed on Saipan and were still fighting there when Admiral Spruance, commanding the Fifth Fleet, received word that the Mobile Fleet under Admiral Ozawa had sortied. Accordingly, Spruance removed all support vessels from the landing zone and prepared for a big fleet engagement.

Superficially, the situation of the U.S. Fifth Fleet at this time resembled that of the Japanese Combined Fleet at Midway. Carrier groups had been detached from Task Force 58 to attack Iwo Jima and Chichi Jima while the rest of that force remained in the vicinity of Saipan to protect the amphibious forces moving into the southern Marianas. At such a critical moment the Japanese Mobile Fleet was approaching to attack the divided elements of the Fifth Fleet.

But there was also an essential difference between Midway and Saipan: the element of surprise, which favored the defenders at Midway, was lacking at Saipan. Through communications intelligence we knew what the Mobile Fleet was up to. As it turned out, I received an important message that revealed the exact position of the Japanese fleet just before both sides locked in combat. Ozawa was evidently worried that his ships might be attacked by the Imperial Navy's own submarines. Unfortunately, Spruance ignored this intercepted message, placing more credence in a garbled U.S. submarine report that gave an incorrect position.

Nothing could alter the fact, however, that the Mobile Fleet was overmatched. American naval superiority was awesome in all departments: 15 U.S. against 9 Japanese carriers, 7 U.S. against 5 Japanese battleships, 21 against 13 cruisers, 69 against 28 destroyers, and 891 U.S. against 430 Japanese carrier planes. In terms of air power the advantage was more pronounced because the U.S. pilots were already veterans while the Japanese were green and untrained.

Ozawa hoped that he could offset this superiority with Japanese land-based aircraft as well as carrier planes that possessed a longer range than their U.S. counterparts. He believed that he could stand off beyond the range of the American planes while the Japanese carrier planes were attacking the U.S. fleet, shuttle bombing the Americans by flying between his carriers and Japanese bases like Tinian and Guam.

The Japanese admiral's optimism proved to be unfounded. His land-based aircraft had been wiped out by U.S. carrier planes and the air bases on Guam and Tinian had been neutralized well in advance of the battle. Ozawa's pilots were not only outnumbered but also outfought; most of his planes were shot down in aerial combat which the American pilots dubbed the "Marianas Turkey Shoot." At the end, the retreating Mobile Fleet had only thirty-five carrier planes left.

Japanese losses were not limited to aircraft. Two carriers, *Taiho* and *Shokaku*, were sunk by U.S. submarines, although the submarines could not wait around to check the results of their attacks, and it was left to communications intelligence to confirm the sinkings. In GZ I personally handled the messages from the Japanese that reported that the two carriers had gone down.

During the exchanges of air attacks between the two fleets the hard-luck *Hiyo* had been sunk by American carrier planes. A year earlier *Hiyo* had been put out of action for many months by the submarine *Trigger*. So three carriers in all had been lost by the Imperial Navy while the United States had emerged without any warship losses from the battle.

Finally, the Mobile Fleet had made a precipitate retreat from the area, allowing the United States to proceed unhindered in the invasion of the southern Marianas, including Guam and Tinian.

The result of all this was that the United States had advanced within striking distance of Japan, cut off the communications of Truk and the rest of the Carolines with the Japanese home islands, and opened the way, after the capture of a few more of the Carolines and Palaus, to the Philippines. There the central Pacific advance would link up with General MacArthur's offensive north from New Guinea.

While the dual advance to the Philippines was drawing ever closer, I continued to read the coded transmissions from Japanese garrisons left far behind enemy lines, on bypassed islands such as Jaluit, Maloelap, Mili, and Wotje, to name only a few. There was something pathetic about these messages. Many of the same islands had strong garrisons and originally held anywhere from six months' to a year's supplies. Cut off from any resupply or reinforcement, they were battered by continual bombing from U.S. planes whose task was to ensure that they would no longer be a factor in the war.

Initially U.S. Seventh Army Air Force planes kept bombing and strafing the islands after February 1944. Following the American occupation of Kwajalein no supply ships reached the Japanese-held islands in the Marshalls. Two submarines succeeded in reinforcing Mili in March of that year, bringing in about seventy tons of food and ammunition, but another submarine that made a supply run to Wotje about the same time was sunk.

Later, U.S. medium bombers and bomb-carrying fighter planes took over the task of attacking the bypassed atolls. After every attack the Japanese garrisons struggled to put air strips back into service, hoping for plane reinforcements that never arrived. The U.S. planes took off from Tarawa, Makin, and other islands, dropped their bombs on the Japanese-held islands, and landed at Majuro for refueling and rearming, then returned to their original point of departure, once again bombing the Japanese islands on the way.

As time went by, available supplies diminished to the point where the supply problem became increasingly urgent for the Japanese garrisons. Toward the end of the war the Japanese spent more time fishing, growing vegetable gardens, and hunting rats for food than carrying out any military duties. Before the surrender many died from starvation, disease, eating poisoned fish, or in air raids.

As new air reinforcements arrived in the central Pacific, these garrisons became live targets for practice bombing. Although the spirit of Japanese troops remained unbroken, I read one message from a Japanese garrison that unwittingly seemed to reflect the ultimate insult:

"Enemy planes flew over the island this morning and dropped leaflets. The leaflets contained the following text—'You are surrounded and cut off from all reinforcements. Your situation is hopeless. Further resistance on your part serves no military purpose. Your only reasonable action is to surrender without delay. If you refuse to surrender, your island will be used as a target for practice bombing.' "

The Japanese commander who originated this message went on: "Our morale has never been higher. We shall fight on to the end, confident that the spirit of unconquerable Japan will prevail over our enemies. May His Imperial Majesty live ten thousand years!"

CHAPTER 9

The Last Throw
of the Dice

ACCORDING to Japanese legend, Emperor Hirohito and his predecessors were direct descendants of the gods and goddesses who had ruled the ancient world. The most important of these divine figures was the beautiful Amaterasu Ōmikami, the Sun Goddess.

Amaterasu's parents started by creating the world before they gave birth to her as the ruler of the universe. She ascended the Ladder of Heaven and cast her golden illumination upon the world. But then, one day, angered beyond endurance by her brother Susanoo, she went off and shut herself up in a cave, leaving the world in darkness. This disturbed the other gods, who finally thought of a scheme to lure Amaterasu out of her cave by playing on her curiosity: on a tree outside her cave they hung a mirror made out of stars and put on a lusty entertainment that induced her to peer out at its reflection.

In due course, because of constant turmoil in the "Land of

Reed Plains," a grandson of Amaterasu was sent down to eradicate insurrection and bring peace and prosperity to the country. Amaterasu gave her grandson some parting presents: priceless jewels, the star mirror that had lured her out of the cave, and a divine sword, which Susanoo had found inside one of the eight tails of an eight-headed serpent he had slain.

Several generations later the descendants of Amaterasu Ōmikami brought forth on earth the first human emperor, Jimmu Tennō, who eventually established his rule in the province of Yamato, which became the center of Japan and gave it its ancient name.

We may laugh at the inclination of the Japanese to accept the divine origin of their emperors. Yet, as children of Western civilization, are we really so superior? Three centuries ago, on seeing the royal barge come down the Thames in pouring rain, Samuel Pepys expressed shock that the king *permitted* the rain to fall upon him. As with the crown in Britain, even in modern times the king or queen also rules "by the grace of God."

In reading the decoded messages, I could easily recognize that the Japanese continued to believe in the possibility of a divine intervention that would save them from defeat. Since Emperor Hirohito was a direct descendant of the all-powerful Amaterasu, the Sun Goddess, such intervention might be expected. After all, Japan had never been defeated in war, and historical precedent for divine intervention already existed. In the thirteenth century a Mongol dynasty had seized the throne of China, and after conquering Korea, Kublai Khan demanded the submission of Japan. When the Japanese refused to submit, they exposed themselves to the most serious threat of invasion they had ever faced up to that time. After several efforts to bring the Japanese into line had failed, Kublai Khan decided that strong measures were necessary. He dispatched a huge expedition in the year 1281. In all probability, Japan would have been conquered had it not been for a great typhoon that wiped out the Mongol armada. To the Japanese, it seemed that they owed their salvation to a divine wind, a *kami-*

kaze. Because of the historical precedent, this name was destined to be remembered in World War II.

The progressive deterioration of the military situation made Japanese leaders fear that an invasion of their home islands was imminent. The immediate threat was to the last defensive chain that protected their communications with areas seized in the south— the Philippines, Taiwan, and the Ryukyus—behind which oil from the East Indies could still be transported to Japan by its dwindling tanker fleet. Once this oil had been cut off, the Japanese war machine would grind to a halt.

These leaders were less sanguine about the outcome of the war than the Japanese people as a whole, and they were also less hopeful about a miracle that could save Japan. Yet they remained equally determined to seek a "general decisive battle." That purpose became the basis for an operational plan drawn up by Imperial General Headquarters.

Significantly, the plan was called Sho-Go ("Victory Operation"), and it had been worked out in four variations: Sho-1 for the Philippines, Sho-2 for Taiwan and the Ryukyus, Sho-3 for Kyushu and Honshu, and Sho-4 for Hokkaido and the Kuriles. The variation that would be activated depended upon the target that the Americans chose to attack.

As it happened, the navy section of Imperial General Headquarters correctly estimated that the next landing would take place in the Philippines in the last ten days of October 1944, probably on the island of Leyte.

Pinpointing the Philippines as the next target was due not so much to reconnaissance as to intelligence sources. One of the most significant of those sources was a diplomatic message to Tokyo from Ambassador Naotake Sato in Moscow on or about October 6; we intercepted it in PURPLE. According to Sato, a source in the Soviet Foreign Ministry had informed him of an Allied "leak" to the effect that U.S. air forces in China had been ordered to attack the Philippines so as to isolate the islands.

Those of us in GZ who read this message wondered why the

USSR, an ally of the United States, would wish to pass such information to an enemy of the United States. We could, of course, only guess at the motives of Soviet representatives. It seemed as if they did not want the United States to achieve an early victory in the Pacific war and hoped to delay a decision until Moscow was ready to enter the war and claim its share of the spoils. Stalin had no real cause for concern: four months later, at the Yalta Conference, Roosevelt and Churchill agreed to his conditions for Soviet entry into the war against Japan—recovery of southern Sakhalin, annexation of the Kurile Islands, and restoration of the lease of Port Arthur as a Soviet naval base coupled with recognition of the USSR's predominant interest in the commercial port of Dairen.

But our urgent concern was with the coming Battle for Leyte Gulf, which turned out to be a series of four major engagements spread over hundreds of miles and involving many more ships than were engaged by the British and German fleets in the Battle of Jutland during World War I.

When the invasion of Leyte began, Admiral Toyoda's Combined Fleet was already widely dispersed. The carrier force with screening vessels commanded by Vice-Admiral Ozawa remained in the Inland Sea, where pilot training could best be conducted, while the heavy surface force under the command of Vice-Adm. Takeo Kurita had been dispatched to Lingga Roads, near Singapore, close to indispensable fuel supplies. A third force of cruisers and destroyers under Vice-Adm. Kiyohide Shima stood at Amami Oshima in the Ryukyus. Admiral Toyoda, commander in chief of the Combined Fleet, was in Tokyo, awaiting developments.

As soon as he heard that American minesweepers were clearing a path into Leyte Gulf, on October 17, Toyoda issued a Sho-1 operational alert to all ships of the Combined Fleet. He waited, however, until the eighteenth, when he was certain about the invasion of Leyte, to issue the "Execute" order for Sho-1, setting October 25 as X-day for the destruction of enemy amphibious forces.

The Sho-1 plan, which we already knew from communications intelligence, was simple enough in its general outline but exceedingly difficult in execution, requiring a high degree of coordination and precise timing.

Ozawa's force of carriers, the Main Body, was to come down from the north and act as bait (like Amaterasu Ōmikami's star mirror) to lure Admiral Halsey's Third Fleet away from the central Philippines where the main action would take place. Ozawa was prepared to sacrifice his carriers for this purpose. *Ise* and *Hyuga*, battleships half converted into aircraft carriers, carried no planes at all. To make the bait more attractive, Ozawa added to the force *Zuikaku*, which had participated in the Pearl Harbor attack, and the light carriers *Zuiho, Chitose,* and *Chiyoda,* for which trained air groups were lacking. So much for the Main Body, which seemed to be something of a misnomer.

While Halsey, it was hoped, dashed off in pursuit of Ozawa's Main Body, one part of Kurita's No. 1 Striking Force, known as the "A" Force, under his direct command, would pass through the center of the Philippines from west to east by way of San Bernardino Strait and turn south to rendezvous at Leyte Gulf with the other part of his command, the "C" Force, under Vice-Admiral Nishimura, which was due to reach Leyte Gulf through the northern entrance of Surigao Strait after a penetration farther south. Vice-Admiral Shima's No. 2 Striking Force was to follow Nishimura through Surigao Strait. At this point the Japanese naval forces, reunited, would destroy the amphibious vessels, fire support ships in Leyte Gulf, and attack the beachhead itself. Thus, in accordance with Toyoda's order to Ozawa, the Main Body of carriers would "advance into the Philippine Sea east of Luzon and lure the enemy to the north," allowing the pincer operation to go forward without interference from Halsey's Third Fleet.

So much for the Sho-1 plan. Ordinarily it should not have had any chance of success, since the Japanese once again had been deprived of the advantage of surprise. However, forewarned is not always forearmed.

In GZ we began to map the progress of the separate Japanese naval forces as they gradually converged on Leyte Gulf in a last desperate gamble—a last throw of the dice—to turn the tide and give the Americans a setback that might win precious time for Japan. In our own efforts we were aided by the fact that the coordination of the various Japanese naval forces depended on good radio communication, and that in turn afforded us the opportunity to follow their movements in detail through our interception and decoding of their messages.

Thus, as the Battle for Leyte Gulf—the final surface battle of the Pacific war—approached, communications intelligence knew all about the three main movements of the Japanese Combined Fleet.

As early as October 23 Admiral Kurita's "A" Force suffered its first losses after being spotted by U.S. submarines in the Palawan Passage. Torpedoes sank the heavy cruiser *Atago* almost immediately, blew up another heavy cruiser, *Maya,* and crippled a third cruiser, *Takao.*

However, Kurita encountered considerably more trouble on the twenty-fourth when U.S. air reconnaissance located his force in the Sibuyan Sea. All that day Third Fleet carrier-based planes attacked the "A" Force in waves. Kurita, who had practically no air cover, kept sending messages asking urgently for air support, but Vice-Adm. Shigeru Fukudome, commanding all land-based aircraft in the Philippines, ignored Kurita's pleas, preferring to unleash his planes against the enemy carriers.

Kurita's force reeled before 259 sorties by American carrier planes. Under this devastating barrage four battleships sustained direct hits while the heavy cruiser *Myoko* was put out of action and retired from the battle. The most dramatic result of these attacks, however, was the sinking of the superbattleship *Musashi,* which had offered a particularly inviting target. *Musashi* staggered under nineteen torpedo and eighteen bomb hits; she finally capsized late in the day and went down with eleven hundred men. In the meantime, the only success Fukudome could chalk up for his planes was the sinking of a U.S. light carrier, *Princeton.*

Thoroughly discouraged by his various setbacks, Kurita sent off a message to Admiral Toyoda, CinC Combined Fleet, informing him that he had been under attack by more than 250 planes. He went on to say, "It is therefore considered advisable to retire temporarily from the zone of enemy air attacks and to resume the advance when the battle results of friendly units permit."

Thus Kurita gave his superior a not very subtle hint that he desperately needed air cover. He ordered his force to retire westward. But he soon realized that he was falling too far behind schedule and therefore ordered the "A" Force to reverse course again and head for San Bernardino Strait.

Admiral Nishimura's "C" Force had been sighted in the Sulu Sea on the morning of the twenty-fourth by U.S. carrier-based planes, and it soon came under attack. At this point, however, the "C" Force was luckier than the "A" Force, suffering only minor damage. The battleship *Fuso* received a hit on her fantail, and the destroyer *Shigure* was hit on a turret. Nishimura grew worried nonetheless and sent a message to Kurita stating that he was encountering difficulties.

As it turned out, Nishimura's force completely escaped attack during the afternoon and evening of the twenty-fourth and was able to make steady progress.

During the evening of the twenty-fourth Admiral Toyoda sent a short message to all fleet elements scheduled to participate in the Sho-1 operation: "All forces will dash to the attack, trusting in divine guidance."

At this stage of the battle the U.S. Navy appeared to have the situation well in hand. Admiral Halsey's Third Fleet was positioned off San Bernardino Strait, from which Kurita's "A" Force had to exit before it could turn south. The Third Fleet also had a blocking position that ensured that the carriers of Ozawa's Main Body, coming down from the north, would have to cope with the superior air strength of that fleet before it could hope to accomplish anything.

To the south, Admiral Kinkaid, commanding the U.S. Seventh Fleet, had already taken steps to deal with Vice-Admiral Nishimura's "C" Force and Vice-Admiral Shima's No. 2 Striking Force.

Kinkaid ordered Adm. Jesse Oldendorf to form a battle line across the northern entrance to Surigao Strait, from which the Japanese would have to emerge on their way to Leyte Gulf.

If the U.S. naval forces had maintained their positions, Toyoda's Combined Fleet would have had virtually no chance to accomplish its mission. But now a completely unexpected factor entered into the equation: the judgment of Admiral Halsey himself. Halsey received word on the afternoon of the twenty-fourth of the location of Ozawa's carrier force, and that evening he surprised almost everyone by taking the whole Third Fleet and pursuing Ozawa, like the leader of a posse who galloped off pell-mell with his men after a few outlaws while the rest of the gang robbed the bank in town. Halsey did not leave even a single destroyer to watch the eastern exit of San Bernardino Strait. This was of course precisely what the Japanese had planned all along. Admiral Kurita's "A" Force could now reach the open sea without hindrance and head for our beachhead on Leyte.

How could this have happened? Halsey must have been informed about the Sho-1 plan. He not only knew that Ozawa's force was a decoy; he also knew that Kurita was still on his way through the center of the Philippines (he had been told about Kurita's reversal of course before he ordered the Third Fleet to go north) and that Nishimura and Shima were coming through in the south. It was true that he had overestimated the success of his carriers' air attacks on the "A" Force, and he also feared that Ozawa might be able to shuttle-bomb his fleet between the carriers and Japanese land bases in the Philippines. Despite all this, he had overwhelming strength at his disposal and could have easily handled both enemy forces at the same time. The truth was that Halsey's ambition was to sink ships and, unfortunately, Nimitz's orders had provided him with a loophole to go his own way.

Admiral Halsey of course had certain attitudes that were common to battle commanders. Like all such commanders, he had to adhere to general orders from his superiors, in this case an Operation Plan issued by Admiral Nimitz, CincPac. Yet all battle commanders rightly retained a flexibility of action and independence of judgment enabling them to make necessary adjustments in the course of combat. As commanders, they prided themselves on their ability to make independent decisions and reject outside influences that seemed likely to impose decisions upon them.

One such influence was intelligence, which they could not control except within narrow limits. Although they wanted to have access to intelligence sources, they had a tendency to be skeptical about such information, which does indeed want to be weighed carefully. They preferred to obtain intelligence through sources more amenable to their control, such as air and submarine reconnaissance. In the final analysis they relied heavily upon their own strategic assessment of the situation and their own tactical calculations. Fitting as this might have been, they were inclined to reject anything that did not agree with their preconceptions.

Examples of this skepticism about intelligence were not hard to find. Despite the fact that we were privy to Yamamoto's plans for the Midway operation from the beginning, Adm. Robert Theobald, who commanded our Aleutian surface forces, rejected the information because he thought that it had been planted by the Japanese. As a result, he chose to ignore Japanese plans to invade the western Aleutians and launch air attacks at Dutch Harbor in the eastern Aleutians for diversionary purposes. Instead he disposed his forces to oppose a landing at Dutch Harbor that was never in the cards. During the Battle of the Philippine Sea Admiral Spruance placed more credence in a garbled (and incorrect) U.S. submarine report concerning the Japanese Mobile Fleet's position than a decoded message that gave its exact position. And finally there was Admiral Halsey's own inclination to follow his instincts by taking off in pursuit of Ozawa's decoy carriers, disregarding communications intelligence that pointed at a coordinated attack of the other Japanese naval forces against Leyte.

Apart from this attitude, which he shared with other commanders, Halsey had personal characteristics that made him an exceedingly tough fighter but not the most cerebral flag officer. He was noted for his aggressiveness and determination together with an impatience that hardly fitted him for a waiting game. The origin of his nickname—"Bull"—could not have been a mystery to anyone who knew him, not even Halsey himself.

At about 2000 hours on October 24, despite his knowledge that Kurita's force was once again headed for San Bernardino Strait, Halsey rejected the idea, as he put it, of "statically" guarding the strait and charged north with his entire fleet in pursuit of Ozawa's carrier force, effectively uncovering the beachhead.

In GZ my colleagues and I continued to plot the movements of the Japanese naval forces with appropriate pins on the charts, unaware of the disposition of our forces except for what the Japanese themselves reported whenever they made contact with the enemy.

At almost the same moment that Halsey was ordering his Third Fleet to steam north, Kurita received separate instructions from CinC Combined Fleet to proceed with the original plans. Kurita had already reversed course to the west, ending his earlier vacillation. But he was not to distinguish himself in this battle. He appeared a typical Japanese admiral, cultivating the samurai look, with scowling face and tightly pressed lips, but with his black eyebrows and bald head which carried a gray stubble, he looked more like a samurai than the others. He wore a plain navy blue uniform with only a single decoration on the breast, the Order of the Chrysanthemum.

Reacting to Toyoda's instructions, Kurita immediately replied: "Main Body No. 1 Striking Force will pass through San Bernardino Strait at 0100 October 25. Estimated time of arrival at Leyte Gulf 1100 hours."

Kurita had also received a message from Nishimura that the latter would transit Surigao Strait and enter Leyte Gulf at 0400 on October 25. Kurita sent word to Nishimura that he would expect to rendezvous with that force ten miles northeast of Suluan Island at 0900 the same day.

Meanwhile Admiral Ozawa had received CinC Combined Fleet's "dash to the attack" message as well as separate instructions on the evening of the twenty-fourth to proceed with the attack as planned. Accordingly, he headed to the southwest and continued with his diversionary operations, doing his utmost to attract Halsey's attention. In this he proved to be all too successful.

At the time Halsey was heading north toward Ozawa with his fast carrier groups and all his battleships and cruisers, Kurita's "A" Force passed through San Bernardino Strait unopposed and even managed to exit into the open sea without being detected.

Nishimura had been lucky thus far, but his good fortune came to an abrupt end. In Surigao Strait, to the south, he ran into disaster for himself and his ships when he encountered the waiting Americans. Unlike Halsey at San Bernardino Strait, Kinkaid was guarding Surigao Strait and had no intention of giving Nishimura free passage.

I saw a message that originated from *Fuso*, one of Nishimura's battleships. *Fuso* reported at about 0300 hours, "We have received two torpedo hits and are unable to make way." At almost the same time the destroyer *Michishio* got off a message that she was sinking while another destroyer, *Asagumo*, reported that she had sustained heavy damage, all from torpedo hits.

At 0330 Nishimura himself sent an urgent battle report: "Enemy torpedo boats and destroyers on both sides of entrance to Surigao Strait. Two of our destroyers torpedoed and drifting. *Yamashiro* sustained one torpedo hit but no impediment to battle cruising."

Strangely enough, Nishimura was apparently unaware that *Fuso*, his other battleship, had also been hit by torpedoes and had already sheered out of the column. In pitch darkness, with a quartering moon that had already disappeared, it was difficult to tell what was happening. Nishimura had his flag on *Yamashiro* and knew about the condition of that ship, but he must have missed *Fuso*'s message. Shortly after Nishimura sent off his own message, *Fuso* exploded into two halves and sank in the course of the next hour or two.

Nishimura had run into a classic naval ambush. In the first

hours after midnight he was attacked by PT boats which he contemptuously brushed aside, like so many flies. But the PT boats slowed him down enough to make his ships that much more vulnerable to the destroyers that dashed in to launch their torpedoes, a number of times with deadly effect.

As he drew closer to the northern entrance to Surigao Strait, Nishimura had only the battleship *Yamashiro,* the heavy cruiser *Mogami,* and the destroyer *Shigure* left in his force. Then Admiral Oldendorf crossed the *T* with his battleships, much as Togo had done to the Russian fleet at Tsushima Strait, and the U.S. cruisers attacked from the flanks.

Nishimura's situation was hopeless. He went down with his flagship *Yamashiro* while *Mogami,* badly wounded, staggered away from the battle zone. The destroyer *Shigure* was destined to be the sole survivor of Nishimura's "C" Force.

Vice-Admiral Shima with his No. 2 Striking Force headed north in Surigao Strait, passing the wreckage of *Fuso* and other ships. Shima thought he was coming to Nishimura's aid, but it soon became apparent that there was nothing to aid, and Shima prudently ordered his force of three cruisers and four destroyers to retire. He sent out a message, notifying the other naval forces of his intentions: "This force has concluded its attack and is retiring from the battle area to plan subsequent action."

Actually all that Shima had attacked were a couple of islands that appeared as two blips on his radar screen. As Shima's force was retiring, the ships came upon the burning *Mogami,* which, by a supreme effort, swung around to get into line.

At the Battle of Midway *Mogami* had collided with another heavy cruiser, *Mikuma,* which eventually went down, but she managed to survive a number of attacks by carrier-based planes. This time *Mogami* became involved in a collision with the heavy cruiser *Nachi,* whose stern was badly damaged.

American surface and air forces pursued the retreating Japanese naval units. Once again *Mogami* proved that she could absorb plenty of punishment, but she did not escape again. When she finally remained dead in the water, a Japanese destroyer dispatched her with a torpedo.

Shima's No. 2 Striking Force, diminished to two heavy cruisers and four destroyers, finally extricated itself. The captain of the destroyer *Shigure*—all that remained of Nishimura's "C" Force—notified Admirals Toyoda and Kurita about the fate of that force: "All ships except *Shigure* went down under gunfire and torpedo attack."

Thus the lower part of the pincer had been cut off. However, there was a surprise in store for Admiral Kinkaid's Seventh Fleet, particularly six escort carriers and their screen of destroyers and destroyer escorts. Suddenly it seemed that the whole Japanese Combined Fleet had turned up in the vicinity of Leyte Gulf. This was of course Kurita's "A" Force, which happened to be formidable enough. Thanks to Halsey, the "A" Force had passed through San Bernardino Strait shortly after midnight and now, in the early morning hours, appeared off Leyte.

Facing apparently certain annihilation, the U.S. escort carriers and destroyers went into action with astonishing aggressiveness. The surface units attacked with torpedoes and gunfire, making smoke for concealment, while the planes from the escort carriers dove at the "A" Force to release their loads.

In the ensuing melee, the U.S. side succeeded in dealing out more punishment than it received—a surprising result considering the greatly superior strength of the enemy. After losing three heavy cruisers in short order, Kurita was in a state of confusion. He could not have been stopped from breaking through into Leyte Gulf, but once again he hesitated. Without air support, he was unable to determine the actual strength of his opposition. As it happened, Oldendorf's heavy surface units were too far away in Surigao Strait to intervene; Halsey had taken himself well to the north and could offer no help. Nonetheless, Kurita judged from the aggressiveness of the enemy ships that they could count on powerful support. After several hours of indecision, Kurita gave up without an effort, deciding it was suicidal to risk his ships in Leyte Gulf without aid from Nishimura and Shima, which, he already knew, would not be forthcoming.

Once his decision had been made, Kurita quickly sent off a message to the commander in chief of the Combined Fleet: "No. 1 Striking Force has abandoned penetration of Leyte Gulf. Proceeding north searching for enemy task force. Will engage decisively, then pass through San Bernardino Strait."

Kurita returned the way he had come, harassed by enemy air attacks. Carrier planes from the Third Fleet joined in the pursuit after Halsey reacted to a message from Nimitz inquiring about the whereabouts of the Third Fleet and belatedly broke off the battle with Ozawa's force. Luckily, the worst had been averted, thanks to the heroic resistance of the escort carriers and their destroyer screen, which were not even expected to take part in the battle. Halsey achieved a hollow victory by sinking four of the decoy carriers, including *Zuikaku*, last survivor of the Pearl Harbor attack. Six of the U.S. Navy's newest and most powerful battleships under his command had not fired a shot.

Kurita saved most of his fleet, but his mission ended in complete failure. As a whole, the Imperial Navy had been shattered by its losses in the Battle for Leyte Gulf. Thereafter the U.S. Navy ruled the Pacific and spent its time supporting landings when not engaged in hunting down remnants of the Japanese fleet, destroying the enemy wherever he could be found.

The struggle for Leyte Island, which was really a struggle for the Philippines, did not end with this last big surface battle. The Japanese did all in their power to send troop reinforcements to Leyte, and for a time there seemed to be a disturbing parallel with Guadalcanal as another "Tokyo Express" went into high gear. Although the United States had landed over 100,000 men on the island, the Japanese could siphon troops from a reservoir of some 350,000 soldiers in the Philippines. We followed the transport of reinforcements to Leyte with close attention. Finally, on or about November 10, we decoded a message revealing that a large convoy was about to leave Manila for Ormoc Bay on Leyte.

The information concerning this convoy was sent to Admiral Halsey for urgent action, and Halsey ordered Rear Adm. Forrest Sherman, temporarily commanding Task Force 38, to destroy the convoy.

Sherman's carrier planes bombed the marus as they neared Ormoc Bay and sank all of the ships. With the exception of a few men who succeeded in swimming ashore, 10,000 troops embarked in the convoy went down with the transports.

From this time on the Japanese effort to reinforce Leyte went steadily downhill, despite adverse monsoon weather which washed out bridges and roads and made the island a sea of mud. The Americans finally concluded the conquest of Leyte by landing troops at Ormoc Bay and completely encircling the enemy forces.

Even before the Battle for Leyte Gulf had taken place, we began to notice references to a "Special Attack Corps" in decoded messages.

"What kind of unit is it?" I asked Phil Cate.

He shook his small gray head and gave me a puckish look. "Just wait. You'll find out."

"It seems to have something to do with planes."

"Planes?" Cate said, raising his thick eyebrows. "How do you know it isn't the V-1 or the V-2?"

He spoke with utmost seriousness, but I knew him well enough to recognize when he was jesting. As he had suggested, we did not have long to wait.

The Special Attack Corps made its first appearance of note on October 25 during the Battle for Leyte Gulf when Kurita's force engaged U.S. escort carriers off Samar. It turned out to be the kamikazes which thereafter instituted a reign of terror for U.S. ships in the concluding phase of the Pacific war. The kamikazes were highly maneuverable Zeke fighters carrying light bombs; inexperienced pilots could fly them on suicide missions, crashing them into our ships, sometimes to horrible effect.

In that first attack off Samar three escort carriers were hit by the kamikazes, one carrier sinking. Thus a new and terrifying

weapon came into being just as the Imperial Navy had been eliminated as a threat. But the kamikazes alone could not seriously
challenge American command of the sea. The "divine wind" of the
thirteenth century was not to be repeated by this "divine wind" of
the twentieth century.

Perhaps Amaterasu herself had grown angry. Whatever the
reason, the Sun Goddess obviously had withdrawn her favor and
did not choose on this occasion to send an emissary to suppress dis-
turbances and insurrection in the "Land of Reed Plains" below.

Downfall

A FTER the invasion of the Philippines and the restoration of
that country's independence as massive Allied naval, land,
and air forces moved ever closer to Japan, the work of GZ
and other components of communications intelligence concerned
with Japan became less vital to the war effort.

Although we were rapidly becoming redundant, we continued
to work with the same diligence as before. There was no shortage
of messages to be read. The Japanese also behaved as if nothing
had changed, continuing to send the same routine dispatches about
rosters and leaves of their men and the thousand and one minutiae
that are the lifeblood of military organizations.

It might have been "business as usual," but by no means all
messages were routine. Judging by communications intelligence,
the Japanese still behaved as if they expected to win the war. The
commanders kept drawing up operational plans for new offensive
operations which bore grandiose names suggesting that some final
or decisive victory would be attained. The composition of the at-

tacking forces as well as the numbers of planes, ships, and other types of armament looked formidable on paper. The Japanese might have been short of fuel, ammunition, or spare parts to keep their equipment operational, but they went over to the attack whenever and wherever they could and fought bitterly and stubbornly even when the odds seemed hopeless. In the process they killed and wounded many of our men. And they gave no sign of knowing or acknowledging what some of our military leaders confidently asserted, that they had been beaten and that the war to all intents and purposes was over.

So work never slackened at the Communications Annex, but much of the excitement of the past had gone out of it. As before, I directed the work of my section and had a number of male officers under my command, but the yeomen all had gone off to sea, replaced by attractive, and occasionally distracting, young WAVE enlisted women. The change, however, had not been limited only to people. There was a less tangible kind of change in the air. We could make a difference where the balance of forces was virtually equal and the struggle could go either way, or when, as at Midway, we could offset superior strength by concentrating all our available forces at the right point and eliminating the element of surprise. Now nothing mattered, for we knew that we possessed the power to overcome Japanese resistance.

Although Japan had fought the Pacific war without the direct help of a single major ally, it was still true that its Axis partners— Hitler's Germany and Mussolini's Italy—seemingly riding the wave of the future in early years, gave potent psychological support while their military situation offered encouragement. Then the tide turned in the fall of 1942, when Soviet armies surrounded the Germans at Stalingrad, the British decisively defeated Rommel at El Alamein, and powerful Allied amphibious forces landed in North Africa. For the Japanese, the hope placed in their partners flickered and was only extinguished in late 1944 and early 1945. By then Italy was, to all intents and purposes, out of the war, and after the failure of Hitler's last gamble, the Christmas offensive in the

Ardennes, the hundreds of divisions of the Western Allies and the Soviet Union were closing in on Germany. Thereafter Japan remained alone, more alone than ever, and its leaders knew that it would only be a matter of time before the enemy shifted in overwhelming force from Europe to the Far East to crush Japan.

Still the drama, like a classical Greek tragedy, had to be played out to its inevitable end. Facing hopeless odds, Japan refused to concede defeat and went on without visible change while we were mapping plans to invade other islands on its very doorstep. As in Saipan, the Japanese were prepared to fight to the last in order to exact the highest price from us. Yet among them there were some Japanese who thought that it made no sense to persist in a useless resistance, recalling a popular saying, *"Baka nimo hodo ga aru"* ("There is a limit even to stupidity").

B-29 bombing raids on Tokyo had commenced in November 1944 from recently captured bases on Saipan, but the distance was so great that it forced a reduction in bomb loads, and because of the lack of fighter protection the B-29s had to bomb from a high altitude with consequent loss of accuracy. In view of these circumstances, American military leaders decided that it was essential to capture Iwo Jima or one of the other Volcano Islands, depriving the Japanese of airfields that could be used for fighter interception of the B-29s and putting the airfields to use by our own fighters. The date for the landing on Iwo Jima was set for February 1945.

The Japanese high command correctly estimated that Iwo Jima would be our next target and set about turning the island into a fortress of forbidding strength. Iwo Jima was little more than a pile of volcanic ash with a plateau wrinkled by rills and crevices on the northeast end of the island and Mount Suribachi, an extinct volcano, on the southern end, offering practically no cover to the attackers, while all the firepower was concentrated on the higher elevations. The Japanese commander had also greatly increased the island's defensive capabilities through mutually supporting pillboxes, blockhouses, tunnels, and trenches, which his men dug ever deeper toward the center of the earth.

It was hardly surprising, therefore, that many weeks of bombing and days of bombardment hardly touched the subterranean fortifications of this island. Nor was it surprising that a conquest that, according to prior calculations, should have been completed in five days actually took nearly a whole month. And we suffered a total of twenty-six thousand casualties—more than three thousand dead and wounded for each square mile of the island's eight square miles of barren volcanic ash. Erected in Washington, D.C., after the war, the statue of marines raising the flag on Mount Suribachi (a smaller version stands at the gate of Marine Corps Headquarters in Quantico, Virginia) provided an enduring reminder of this terrible sacrifice.

Before our planned invasion of the Japanese home islands could take place in the fall of 1945, we needed to seize Okinawa, providing ourselves with closer air bases to support the invasion. Iwo Jima had given us only a foretaste of what was to come on Okinawa, a larger and more strongly defended island only 350 miles from Japan.

Even so, the fierceness of the opposition we encountered was probably on a scale we could not have anticipated. When U.S. forces invaded Okinawa on April 1, 1945, there was a garrison of more than 100,000 troops waiting to receive them, while all Okinawan civilians who were not needed by the armed forces had been evacuated to the northern part of the island or to Japan. Moreover, in the course of the next weeks the Japanese threw everything they could muster in the way of air power, especially kamikazes, and their remaining sea power at the attackers.

Learning from their past failures in opposing other island invasions, the Japanese had abandoned the practice of trying to wage a decisive battle on the beaches in order to wipe out the invaders as they landed. Instead they chose now to fortify themselves in well-prepared positions inland beyond the range of the big guns of American battleships and cruisers.

On Okinawa Lt. Gen. Mitsuru Ushijima, commanding the defending forces, had concentrated most of his troops in a rugged area of steep hills and deep ravines northeast of Naha, the capital city, and constructed a veritable spider's web of fortifications where he planned to make his final stand.

The Okinawan campaign involved the bloodiest fighting of the whole war up to that time. The war correspondent Ernie Pyle, who had gone through the North African and Italian campaigns without injury, was among those killed. The fighting was bloody not only on land but at sea, where our ships took a horrible battering by kamikazes. One of the worst days was April 6, when the Japanese sent more than 350 kamikazes to attack Task Force 58 off Okinawa, damaging some 22 naval ships and sinking a number of other vessels.

GZ contributed to a particularly weird episode of the war that took place at this time. Not content with having kamikazes fly their suicide missions in the air, the Japanese leadership resorted to kamikazes in the water.

We broke a message that ordered a force consisting of the superbattleship *Yamato,* the light cruiser *Yahagi,* and eight destroyers to sortie from Kure in the Inland Sea on April 6 and proceed to Okinawa, arriving at dawn on April 8. There the ships were to beach themselves and fire at the American forces until their ammunition had been exhausted or they had been destroyed. As we learned later, these ships received the last twenty-five hundred tons of fuel oil in Japan—barely enough for a *one-way* trip to Okinawa.

This information from GZ was rushed to Admiral Spruance's Fifth Fleet, and Spruance promptly ordered a battleship force to prepare to intercept the enemy force. Admiral Mitscher, however, had no intention of standing by idly while the battleships went into action. He sent out search planes from his Task Force 58, and when they discovered the enemy ships early on April 7, he ordered a number of air groups to attack immediately.

Waves of the carrier-based planes delivered devastating blows around noon, giving the huge *Yamato* special attention. *Yamato,* at 64,000 tons one of the largest battleships ever built (along with her sister ship, *Musashi,* sunk in the Battle for Leyte Gulf), had 18-inch guns firing a 3,200-pound projectile. But she was helpless before the ceaseless attacks of the carrier planes and, after absorbing enormous punishment, rolled over and sank in less than two hours. The use of *Yamato* as a kamikaze ship was like the sacrifice in chess of a queen, the most powerful piece on the chessboard, to prevent checkmate of the king—and just about as futile. It seemed somehow appropriately symbolic that *Yamato,* bearing the ancient name of Japan and carrying the flag of the Rising Sun, should have gone to her watery grave in this final phase of the war.

Mitscher's pilots also sank the light cruiser *Yahagi* and two destroyers while damaging two other destroyers so badly that they were later sunk by the surviving ships. Only four destroyers out of the whole force escaped the fury of U.S. air attacks and managed to return to safety in the Inland Sea.

Less than a week later, on Thursday, April 12—while the Okinawan campaign followed its bloody course—the war was overshadowed for the moment by the shocking news of a great man's death, which seemed to dramatize far more than all the battles not just the tragedy of our times but also the mortality affecting great and small alike.

I was off duty that day and played a round of golf in the afternoon at Bannockburn, Maryland. As I came home toward evening, I could hear the radios with their volumes turned up in the houses I passed, much as I remembered on that other day, the Sunday of Pearl Harbor.

When I came into our apartment, my wife met me at the door. "The president is dead," she said.

We sat down in the living room, unable to speak, and listened to the hushed voices on the radio.

In his bunker in Berlin, under the guns of approaching Russian armies, Adolf Hitler, who saw himself as a man born under a lucky star, was overjoyed by the news of Roosevelt's death. He and Joseph Goebbels celebrated the occasion, which they both saw as the miracle for which Hitler had been waiting. But the Japanese

18. Japan's superbattleship *Yamato* shown fleeing from aerial bombs and torpedoes, April 7, 1945. Although burning amidships, she was still able to make ten to fifteen knots when this photo was taken.

leaders, who had never regarded Roosevelt as an archenemy and personal devil, possessed a more realistic view concerning the significance of his death. They knew that it would make no difference in the waging of the war, and they were resigned to fighting the war to the finish.

It took close to three months for the United States to complete its conquest of Okinawa. By the time the island was secured, the opposing generals had died, Gen. Simon Buckner being killed in action, General Ushijima by ceremonial suicide (*seppuku*, or as it was incorrectly called in the West, "harakiri"). Around 100,000 Japanese troops had been killed (there were only 11,000 prisoners

19. A huge explosion aboard the *Yamato*, resulting from the repeated attacks by U.S. planes, stopped her dead in the water. *National Archives.*

of war) and at least 25,000 Okinawan civilians, caught in the fighting, were also killed, while about 13,000 Americans lost their lives. Kamikazes alone had exacted the frightening toll of 26 Allied ships sunk and 368 damaged.

Even before the fighting on Okinawa ended, U.S. military leaders began laying plans for the invasion of Japan. In April the Joint Chiefs of Staff ordered Nimitz and MacArthur to "make plans and preparations for the campaign in Japan." In earlier planning the invasion had already been given the code name Downfall. The planners had divided Downfall into two stages: first of all, Operation Olympic, the invasion of the southern island of Kyushu, to be followed by Operation Coronet, the invasion of Honshu, the main island, where Japan's capital, Tokyo, and most of its major cities were located.

In spite of this, the Joint Chiefs still hesitated. They could not be certain how soon the fighting in Europe would end. There were the logistical problems of redeploying troops and equipment from Europe to the Pacific, of concentrating shipping, and of establishing staging bases. And there were other imponderables, such as the question of Soviet entry into the Pacific war as well as the effectiveness of the atomic bomb, which the Manhattan Project had not yet tested.

It still remained to be seen whether Japan could be induced to surrender without an invasion of the home islands. The loss of Saipan in July 1944 had led to the fall of General Tojo's essentially military government. Some observers took the change of government as a sign that Japan wished to sue for peace. The new premier, Kuniaki Koiso, had established a Supreme War Council which, he hoped, would function as a link between the cabinet and the high command. But the new leaders were unable to come up with any new proposals that would also satisfy the military, and therefore there could be no positive moves toward peace.

In February 1945 Emperor Hirohito met with a group of elder statesmen to examine possible steps to achieve peace. Meanwhile the war situation continued to deteriorate. Japan had been brought within the range of the B-29s after the U.S. conquest of Saipan, and in 1945 extensive firebomb raids ravaged every one of Japan's major cities with the exception of the ancient capital of Kyoto, which was more like a museum, filled with unique wooden architecture, lovely palaces, and moated castles, with priceless antiquities.

Despite the hopelessness of the situation, some Japanese leaders, especially in the military, found compelling reasons for continuing the war. The Allied insistence on unconditional surrender, which seemed to exclude the possibility that the emperor could be preserved, was a condition for ending the war and offered a handy excuse: after all, only the emperor had any influence over the military, but he could not urge them to make peace if he himself did not remain a symbol of unity capable of saving the country from chaos. The military also continued to hope for a major victory or a protracted, indecisive struggle as a means of obtaining more favorable conditions for ending the war.

An additional problem was the Japanese people, who had been assured all along that Japan was winning the war. As early as the Battle of Midway, the leadership had concealed all news of the defeat from the people. At later stages of the war the military leaders continued to make extravagant claims of victory. For example, when Admiral Halsey's Third Fleet conducted devastating raids on Formosa just before the invasion of Leyte, without losing a single ship, the navy section of Imperial General Headquarters issued an official communiqué on October 16, 1944, claiming a great Japanese victory: the sinking of eleven carriers, two battleships, three cruisers, and one destroyer or light cruiser; the damaging of eight carriers, two battleships, four cruisers, one destroyer or light cruiser, and thirteen other ships; and, finally, a dozen other ships set afire. The whole nation joined in a delirious celebration of this victory. Hirohito himself issued an imperial rescript. Public celebrations of the "Glorious Victory of Taiwan" took place all over Japan as well as at military installations in Formosa and the Philippines. After misleading the people in this manner, few of the same leaders had the stomach to inform the country of Japan's defeat.

After the U.S. invasion of Okinawa the Koiso government fell and a new government headed by Adm. Kantarō Suzuki came to power, knowing that it was not a question of *whether* but rather *when* Japan would make peace.

While the new Japanese government was trying to think of a way to placate military extremists and still end the war, the U.S. Joint Chiefs of Staff had under consideration various options that were still open even at the time they took the first tentative steps toward an invasion of Japan.

The first alternative, obviously, was the execution of the Downfall plan for an invasion; the second was to try to prepare for the Downfall plan by extending conquests westward to positions in

China and Korea that could be useful for the invasion, simultaneously softening up the targets of Kyushu and Honshu; and the third alternative, a combination of air force and navy thinking, envisaged the gradual strangulation of Japan by strategic bombing from the air and a naval blockade of its coasts, hopefully bringing about an early surrender without an invasion.

Following Nazi Germany's collapse in May 1945, the Joint Chiefs of Staff leaned more and more toward invasion, and they set target dates in November for Operation Olympic, the invasion of Kyushu, and March for Operation Coronet, the invasion of Honshu.

In Operation Olympic three corps would be landed in southern Kyushu to seize the area around Kagoshima Bay before advancing to the north and capturing the rest of the island. With the support of air bases on Kyushu, Operation Coronet could then go forward on Honshu, with Gen. Robert Eichelberger's Eighth Army landing at Sagami Bay to seize Yokohama and bypass Tokyo, while Gen. John Hodge's First Army went ashore on Honshu's east coast and advanced across the Kanto Plain toward Tokyo and the east shore of Tokyo Bay.

In accordance with directives of the Joint Chiefs of Staff, General MacArthur, who was the logical choice to lead the armies conducting the invasion, and Admiral Nimitz, who would be responsible for the amphibious operations against Japan, began to take the first steps toward a victorious conclusion of the war.

In that summer of 1945 all of us in GZ were carefully studying Japanese coded messages for concrete indications of an intention to seek peace. For a long time we found nothing of a positive nature. Then, suddenly, without any forewarning, like a streak of lightning stabbing downward in a clear blue sky, the news we were looking for burst upon us from an old source we had forgotten for many, many months—Magic, which, in spite of all that had happened, had not lost its capacity to surprise and enchant all those who came within its reach.

CHAPTER 11

The End of a Time of Troubles

ARNOLD Toynbee once wrote: "A universal state is not the first stage in the disintegration of a civilization, any more than it is the last. While it is followed by an interregnum, a universal state is preceded . . . by a 'Time of Troubles' that seems usually to occupy several centuries; and if we in our generation were to permit ourselves to judge by the purely subjective criterion of our own feeling about our own age, the best judges among us would probably declare unanimously that our 'Time of Troubles' has undoubtedly descended upon us in our Western World of today. . . ."

There is some question whether the Second World War fitted Toynbee's definition of a Time of Troubles; certainly, however, one could observe a superficial resemblance that seemed to be borne out by the first outline of a new American empire about to take shape after the war, a "universal state" which, according to Toynbee, gave a misleading impression of strength when, in fact, in the long history of civilizations it was a further step in the disintegration of a civilization inevitably to be followed by another Time of Troubles.

After the collapse of Nazi Germany in May 1945 and the redeployment of Allied power against Japan, which appeared certain to bring that country to its knees in the very near future, voices could already be heard, voices that spoke confidently of an American century. As yet no one had applied the term *superpower* to the United States of America, but if anyone had, he would not have been likely to place the Soviet Union in the same category. Aware of U.S. military might, which reached a peak in the atomic bomb, many Americans assessed the future in a mood of boundless optimism.

Yet the American military leadership, much more aware of real and potential U.S. strength than citizens at large, looked upon the final phase of the war in the Far East with considerable apprehension and fear. The projected invasion of the Japanese home islands designed to bring the war to a close would meet, these leaders felt, with unparalleled resistance by defenders eager to exact the last drop of blood before they were killed themselves.

The main island of Okinawa, with no thick forest, no tall grass, no tangled undergrowth, without lakes or mountains, lacking all but the smallest rivers and having many open plains, did not offer favorable defensive terrain, yet over 100,000 Japanese who eventually became casualties had fought so bitterly that the invading American soldiers and marines suffered 50,000 casualties, one-fourth of them dead. Two Japanese generals had ceremoniously committed suicide at the last while whole units of their men lined up and killed themselves with hand grenades rather than surrender.

Japan's topography bore a certain resemblance to that of Italy (ignoring the fact that the one was made up of islands and the other happened to be a peninsula). Both had mountains sloping down into the sea, and level ground was hard to find apart from Japan's Kanto Plain and Italy's Po Valley. Those who recalled the horrors the Italian campaign held for the Allies did not require much imagination to envisage how costly a fanatical defense by Japanese troops could make an invasion of the home islands.

In those islands, some anticipated, one million well-trained and well-equipped Japanese soldiers would resist the invaders by fighting for every foot of ground, availing themselves of the rugged mountain terrain, the forested regions traversed by few roads, and every cavern and hole, every river barrier. How high would our casualties go? Ten times, twenty times those of Okinawa?

For reasons of this kind, the generals had wholeheartedly supported the initiative taken by Roosevelt with Churchill's approval at the Yalta Conference in February 1945 in offering Stalin territorial concessions in the Far East in exchange for Stalin's pledge to enter the war against Japan two or three months after the surrender of Germany. The military believed that Soviet participation in the war offered the only hope for reducing Allied casualties in the Götterdämmerung that would end the war with Japan.

The American attitude changed radically between Yalta and Potsdam. The Yalta Conference was the last summit meeting in which President Roosevelt participated. The change, however, was not only one of personalities. By early July, just before the Potsdam Conference, all the factors entering into American calculations about the course of the war added up to an early victory over Japan. Not only had Japan been driven back to the home islands, but firebomb attacks at night on Japanese cities had achieved astonishing results. In one such attack roughly a quarter of Tokyo, composed to a large degree of wooden buildings, had burned to the ground. Aerial reconnaissance confirmed that the damage to Japanese cities far exceeded the most optimistic American expectations.

Then GZ received some information that also had an important bearing on the conclusion of the war. It came to us in the same Magic that had cast such a spell over everyone who had seen it in that time before Pearl Harbor, which now seemed so distant.

Shortly before the Potsdam Conference, a GY watch officer at the Naval Communications Annex took a message off the teleprinter. It had been intercepted on the Tokyo-Moscow circuit. Reading its contents, we immediately grasped its significance. This was the first indication from any source that the Japanese were thinking seriously of suing for peace. Up to that time there had been a great deal of speculation about their intentions, but, by all appearances, they were determined to fight a suicidal, last-ditch struggle even in the home islands—a prospect from which our military leaders shrank in view of the blood we ourselves would shed.

The message to Moscow was clear. Foreign Minister Togo in Tokyo instructed Japan's ambassador to the Soviet Union, Naotake Sato, to make an urgent request for a meeting with Soviet Foreign Minister Vyacheslav Molotov before the latter's departure to attend the summit meeting at Potsdam. Togo told Sato to inform Molotov of the emperor's strong desire for peace. The only obstacle to a prompt cessation of hostilities was the Allied insistence on Japan's unconditional surrender. The Japanese government, continued Togo, could not agree to this if it meant the abdication of the emperor or an end to the monarchy.

According to Togo, Japan had always respected its Treaty of Neutrality with the Soviet Union. Japan also recognized that the USSR's alliance with the Western powers in the war against Germany gave the USSR a special relationship with the same states that were at war with Japan. In recognition of these facts, Japan fervently wished to obtain the Soviet Union's good offices in mediating an end to the war in the Far East, which, following on the recent conclusion of the European war, would finally restore peace to the world.

Additional messages during the next days only served to clarify the Japanese government's position. On the one hand, the cabinet in Tokyo was trying to play on the Allied fear of a suicidal last stand—a fear that the cabinet itself shared: the ministers knew that the military wanted to fight to the end and presented irreconcilable opposition to peace efforts, possibly aborting the civilian leaders' last-minute efforts to stop the war before Japan was literally razed to the ground. The only hope that the military would acquiesce in peace, they believed, was a surrender based on the authority of the emperor, which was also the only hope of saving the country from complete disintegration.

On the other hand, the Japanese government knew that the United States had obtained a commitment from Stalin to enter the war after Germany's surrender. That time had now arrived. Large numbers of Soviet troops with their equipment were even then being transferred to the Far East over the Trans-Siberian Railway.

Foreign Minister Togo's allusion to the Treaty of Neutrality with the Soviet Union was in itself ironic. This treaty had been concluded by the then Foreign Minister Yosuke Matsuoka in April 1941 at a time when, perhaps, the Japanese government believed that the Berlin-Rome-Tokyo Axis might become a quadripartite alliance that included Moscow. Nevertheless, after the German attack on the USSR, Japan had seriously considered breaking the neutrality pact on several occasions by launching an attack on the Soviet Union in the Far East.

Ambassador Sato complied with his instructions to see Molotov and convey Japan's request for Soviet mediation. Reading the various Japanese Foreign Ministry cables, I wondered what kind of action the Soviet government would take. Certainly it appeared to me and my colleagues in GZ that the least the Soviet leaders could do would be to inform the U.S. and British governments of the Japanese peace feelers. Yet we were not exactly surprised when the Soviet government remained silent. Moscow failed to inform Ambassador Averell Harriman or the State Department in Washington, and Stalin did not communicate with Truman. Obviously the Soviet Union was not interested in a quick peace in the Far East.

Truman, already en route to Potsdam aboard the heavy cruiser *Augusta*, received a briefing on the latest intercepted messages. I did not hear how Truman reacted to this news. His view that Soviet participation in the war against Japan was not only unnecessary but undesirable must have been strengthened. On July 17, by the time the Potsdam Conference opened, he had even more reason to hold to the same view, for he received word that the atomic bomb test had been a complete success.

With the Japanese government already suing for peace and the unprecedented power of the atomic bomb now in American hands, the United States could manage very well without any help from the USSR's massed armies. Indeed, as Europe had already shown, Soviet involvement could only create enormous new problems. The USSR would not be satisfied with the territorial concessions agreed to at Yalta but would also demand a role in the occupation of Japan. We could already see what was happening in Germany because of the USSR's role in the occupation of that country. The United States planned to have its forces occupy parts of Japan, and if Soviet troops were to occupy other parts, there was no telling what the final consequences might be.

Churchill, who had always distrusted the Bolsheviks, and Truman, who had learned to distrust them, came to an early understanding on the undesirability of the USSR's entry into the war with Japan. Their position was awkward, however, since they could hardly seek to undo the agreements made at Yalta, and, moreover, Stalin did not need their concurrence in order to enter the war, being fully determined to do so, whether they liked it or not, so as to obtain the spoils already promised to him.

Thus, while Truman and Churchill were practicing their deceit on Stalin by breaking the news about the atom bomb without *really* telling him (this effort proved to be wasted because Stalin already knew all about the Manhattan Project from his own agents, like Klaus Fuchs and the Rosenbergs), Stalin practiced some deceit of his own about the Japanese government's peace feelers.

In his personal narrative of the Second World War, Churchill described events at the Potsdam Conference and recalled:

> Earlier in the week Stalin had told me privately that as his party was leaving Moscow an unaddressed message had been delivered to him through the Japanese Ambassador. It was presumably meant for either himself or President Kalinin or other members of the Soviet

Government, and was from the Japanese Emperor. It stated that Japan could not accept "unconditional surrender," but might be prepared to compromise on other terms. Stalin had replied that as the message contained no definite proposals the Soviet Government could take no action. I explained to the President that Stalin had not wished to tell him direct lest he might think that the Russians were trying to influence him towards peace. . . .

Having remained silent up to this point, why did Stalin mention the matter at all? Was it really delicacy on his part that kept him from raising the question with Truman or, for that matter, with any other Americans? Stalin was noted for his cunning, but hardly for his diplomacy. Deviousness, yes; tact, no. Of course no one could easily guess the motives of a man like Stalin. Perhaps he remembered Sumner Welles's blunder on the eve of Nazi Germany's attack on the USSR, betraying to the Soviet ambassador the fact that we had broken the Japanese diplomatic code. Possibly he had reason to suspect that we were still reading the code. By mentioning the subject to Churchill, he neatly sidestepped an accusation of bad faith that might have been based on his earlier silence, just as Truman avoided a similar accusation with his "casual" mention to Stalin that the United States possessed a new, extremely powerful weapon (without naming the atomic bomb).

Bomb or no bomb, Stalin was determined to enter the war, and the American leaders remained equally determined to make no further concessions to the USSR or to allow Moscow to play more than a token role in the postwar occupation.

Events were moving quickly in any case. Ignoring the USSR, Truman, Clement Atlee (who had replaced Churchill as prime minister in the meantime), and Chiang Kai-shek issued the Potsdam Declaration—an ultimatum to Japan calling for immediate unconditional surrender.

Ten days later, on August 6, as the Japanese government still procrastinated, the first atomic bomb was dropped on Hiroshima. The second atomic bomb fell on Nagasaki on August 9. On August

14 the Japanese government was ready to accept the terms of "unconditional surrender," although by implication the Allied governments agreed to retain the emperor.

The Soviet Union obviously wanted its rights as a belligerent, declaring war on Japan on August 8, two days after Hiroshima's devastation by an atomic bomb and less than a week before the Japanese surrender.

So the war came to an end. The contribution of our Japanese code-breaking effort to victory is hard to assess, though few knowledgeable people can doubt that it considerably shortened the war in the Pacific and even helped to defeat Germany.

General Marshall wrote Gov. Thomas Dewey in 1944:

> Our main basis of information regarding Hitler's intentions in Europe is obtained from Baron Oshima's messages from Berlin reporting his interviews with Hitler and other officials. . . . These are still in the codes involved in the Pearl Harbor events. . . .
>
> Operations in the Pacific are largely guided by the information we obtain of Japanese deployments. We know their strength in various garrisons, the rations and other stores continuing available to them, and what is of vast importance, we check their fleet movements and the movements of their convoys. The heavy losses reported from time to time which they sustain by reason of our submarine action, largely result from the fact that we know sailing dates and routes of the convoys, and can notify our submarines to lie in wait at the proper points. . . .

I can only add to General Marshall's assessment that our nearly complete knowledge of Japanese intentions and plans provided us with the means of frustrating them while our information from decoded messages enabled us to strike where the enemy was weakest and where, more often than otherwise, he did not expect us.

In the closing period of the war GZ had changed almost beyond recognition. Some time earlier Capt. Rosey Mason had obtained his long-sought command at sea, a navy transport, and departed on his way to becoming an admiral. Other familiar faces had also departed while a few new faces appeared without making much of an impression.

Shortly after the atomic bombs were dropped on Hiroshima and Nagasaki and Japan surrendered, one high-ranking admiral made an inspection of OP-20-G. As he moved through GZ, barely listening to explanations of its operations, an escorting officer remarked in reference to the atomic bomb project, "Well, Admiral, that was two billion dollars well spent."

The admiral snorted. "Yes," he said in a booming voice, "but think of how many battleships we could have built for that money."

Even after the disasters that had overtaken the battleship in World War II, the navy still had a few "battleship admirals" left.

Those of us who remained in GZ had little to do beyond conducting research studies that might be useful at some time in the distant future or simply retiring material to the archives. All Japanese code breaking had of course come to a stop as the U.S. occupation regime replaced Japanese governmental organs and the Japanese armed forces were being demobilized.

In the months that followed the surrender we had to await developments, either to go on to other work or to retire to civilian life. Many of the professors who, as the saying went, had come aboard at the Naval Communications Annex and donned uniforms "for the duration" now waited eagerly for demobilization so that they could return to Harvard, Yale, Princeton, or dozens of other academic institutions across the country.

A number of those who had graduated from the U.S. Navy Japanese language program received invitations to participate in the United States Strategic Bombing Survey in Japan. I weighed the matter for some time before asking for a very different assignment, but Sy Millstein and other friends agreed to take part in the survey.

My own thinking looked more toward the postwar world. It did not take much prescience to see from the conflicts that we were already having with the Soviet Union that peace did not promise to be very durable; on the contrary, the portents suggested that we could not even expect the decade or so of virtual absence of war threats that followed the First World War.

For my part, I was already convinced that the Soviet leaders—cynical, ruthless, unprincipled men with the same kind of conditioning that the Nazi bosses had had—would not hesitate to take advantage of any weakness we displayed to improve their power position and, if possible, get the upper hand over the so-called bourgeois world. As Lenin had suggested, it was only necessary to give the capitalists a spade and they would dig their own graves.

In the light of such an international situation, which threatened to get worse as time went by, I decided that I wanted to prepare myself to make a further contribution to the nation's security. Therefore I asked for an assignment to the U.S. Navy language school in Boulder, Colorado, where Russian had already been taught for several years.

That winter I set out in my car under grim, gray skies heavy with the threat of snow and drove away from Washington over icy secondary roads. As I drove on, the snow began to fall and the roads became even more treacherous. The Pennsylvania Turnpike, which had been reserved for military traffic during the war, still remained closed to civilian vehicles, and I had no alternative but to go up and down over mountains, skidding in places and hardly able to stay on the road, throughout the daylight hours.

Toward dusk I finally came down into Uniontown, Pennsylvania, where I had planned to spend the night. I was exhausted, cold, and depressed as I finally found a place by a factory wall where I could park my car. The temperature had fallen so far below freezing that I doubted I would be able to start the car the next morning and head farther west.

But at that moment I did not care. I was glad to find a hotel room, eat a light supper—in spite of my hunger I had lost my appetite—and climb into a warm bed. Before I fell asleep, I thought about the fact that we had put our Time of Troubles with Japan behind us but were already faced with a bigger, possibly more menacing, Time of Troubles with the Soviet Union. Would our system of government survive? Would *we* survive? I had no way of knowing the answer to such questions. Yet as I felt myself drifting off into a warm cocoon of sleep, caring nothing for the freezing cold that awaited me the next day, I grew certain that I would be there, doing my utmost to confront our enemies and keep them from overcoming us because of our own predilection for being careless and indifferent.

In defining the theme of his final volume of World War II memoirs, Churchill expressed, perhaps better than anyone else, the fear that lay at the root of these thoughts: "How the Great Democracies Triumphed, and so were able to resume the Follies which had so nearly cost them Their Life."

Nevertheless, it seemed to me that the very weaknesses that threatened the existence of Western democracies gave them a unique flexibility in responding to dangerous challenges. I did not regard this as an adequate excuse or justification for such weaknesses, but if democracy itself had to be compromised in order to eliminate them, the cure would be worse than the disease.

An authoritarian regime was like a stick that appeared strong and unyielding but snapped under heavy pressure. A democracy, which often gave an impression of weakness, readily bent but could withstand enormous pressure without breaking.

Speaking for myself, I would join with others who shared the same concern and try to find the correct response to the challenges we were certain to meet in the world of tomorrow.

Index

Akagi (carrier), 46, 96–97, 101
Akashi Maru (ship), 156–57, 158
Akikaze (ship), 156–57
Aleutian Islands, 88, 162
Amaterasu Ōmikami (sun goddess), 178–79, 182, 193
Anthony, Dave, 33–34
Aoba (cruiser), 122
Ardennes offensive, 195–96
Arnold, Gen. Henry, 122
Asagumo (destroyer), 188
Asano (feudal lord), 134, 135
Atago (cruiser), 183
Atlantic, Battle of the, 153, 159
Atlee, Clement, 211
Attu Island, 162
Augusta (cruiser), 209
Australia, 4, 37, 43, 84, 85, 86, 106, 127

Barbey, Adm. Daniel, 132
Bataan, 40
Belleau Wood (carrier), 166
Berlin-Rome-Tokyo Axis, 209
Betio Island, 166
Bismarck Islands, 73, 166
Black, Bill, 40
Borton, Hugh, 14
Bougainville Island, 137, 147
Bradford, John, 52
Brotherhood, Lt. Francis M., 49, 80
Buckner, Gen. Simon, 200
Bukens, Larry, 26
Butaritari Islands, 166–67

Callaghan, Adm. William, 127
Cammann, Schuyler ("Ki"), 33–34, 75, 120
Cape Esperance, 130, 133
Caroline Islands, 114, 165, 171, 175
Cate, Phil, 53, 63, 71, 73, 108
Chiang Kai-shek, 27, 60, 120–21, 211
Chichi Jima, 172, 174
Chikuma (cruiser), 124, 162
China, 20, 26, 27, 43, 75, 120, 179, 204
Chinese Communists, 27, 121
Chinese language, 26
Chitose (carrier), 182
Chiyoda (carrier), 182
Churchill, Winston, 11, 126, 181, 207, 210–11, 215
cipher machines, 54–69
 beginning of, 54–55
 distribution of code books and, 74
 principle of, 54–55
 work in code breaking, 80–83
Columbia University, 14
convoy system, 154–61, 191
 Grand Escort Command Headquarters, 160–61
Coral Sea, Battle of the, 85–87, 92, 103, 124, 154, 164
Corregidor, 84, 86
Cory, Ralph, 52–53, 68–69, 109–12
cryptanalysts, 7
cryptography, 76
Currier, Lt. Pres, 71

Dennis, Betsey, 27, 37
Dennis, Reid, 27
Dewey, Thomas E., 103, 212
Dictionary of Chinese-Japanese Characters (Rose-Innes), 96
disinformatsiya (or "disinformation"), 113
Doolittle, Lt. Col. Jimmy, 42
Dōshisha University, 29
Downfall plan, 201, 203–4
Dutch East Indies, 2, 20, 40, 62, 73, 152, 180
Dutch Harbor, 88, 94, 186

Echigo clan, 134
Edgers, Mrs. Dorothy, 53–54, 63–64, 71
Eichelberger, Gen. Robert, 204
Eighth U.S. Army, 204
Eisenhower, Gen. Dwight D., 127
El Alamein, Battle of, 195
Elisséeff, Serge, 34–36
Engebi Island, 171
ENIGMA cipher machine, 55, 169
Eniwetok Atoll, 170, 171
Enterprise (carrier), 92, 101–2, 114, 115, 118, 123, 126–27, 128
Espiritu Santo Island, 128

"February 26 Incident" (Japan), 136–37
Fiji Islands, 85, 106
First Convoy Escort Fleet, 154
First Japanese Amphibious Brigade, 171
First Japanese Mobile Fleet, 173
First U.S. Army, 204
Fishel, Wes, 33, 40
Fletcher, Adm. Frank Jack, 85, 86, 114–15
Formosa. *See* Taiwan
FRUPAC (Fleet Radio Unit, Pacific), 155

Fuchs, Klaus, 210
Fukudome, Vice-Adm. Shigeru, 183
Fuso (battleship), 184, 188, 189

Germany, 111, 120, 153, 169, 195–96, 204, 206, 209, 211
invasion of U.S.S.R. by, 58–61, 70, 71, 209
Gilbert Islands, 73, 164, 165, 166, 169–71
Gindlin family, 67
go (Japanese chess), 140
Goebbels, Joseph, 199
Goettge, Colonel, 110, 111
Grand Escort Command Headquarters, 160–61
Great Britain, 5, 62, 139
Greater East Asia Coprosperity Sphere, 152
Grew, Joseph Clark, 42–43, 57–58, 119
Gripsholm (liner), 29, 119
GRU. *See* Soviet Military Intelligence
Guadalcanal campaign, 104–33, 141, 143, 145–46, 154, 164
aerial reconnaissance and, 106
American air power and, 117–18, 129–30
garrisons in, 107
interrogation of Japanese prisoners in, 110, 131
Japanese reinforcements in, 113–14
landing beach in, 109–10
location of, 105
Nezumi operations in, 116
OP-20-GZ operations and, 114–25, 133
results of, 132–33
tactical victory in, 124–25
"Tokyo Express" operations in, 116, 126
U.S. mastery of the sea and, 117–18

INDEX

Guam Island, 73, 174–75
GZ operations. *See* OP-20-GZ operations

Hagelin cipher machine, 55
Hainan Maru (ship), 156–57
Hall, Jack, 28–29, 39, 43–44, 47–48, 66
Hall, Robin, 48, 66
Halsey, Adm. William, 123, 124, 126, 145, 148, 192, 203
    Battle for Leyte Gulf and, 180, 184–87, 190, 191
    nickname of, 187
    personal characteristics of, 186–87
Hara, Adm. Chuichi, 164
Harakiri, 200
Harriman, Averell, 209
Haruna (battleship), 122–23, 162
Harvard University, 24–45
Hebern (inventor), 55
Hebern cipher machine, 55
Henderson Field (Guadalcanal), 115, 116, 122, 123, 126, 127, 128, 130, 133, 145–46
Hiei (battleship), 127–28, 129
Hindmarsh, Comdr. Albert, 23, 27
hiragana (phonetic alphabet), 18
Hirohito, Emperor, 178, 179, 202, 203
Hiroshima, atomic bombing of, 211–12, 213
Hiryu (carrier), 46, 98, 100, 101
Hisai-san, 16, 17, 18–19, 29
Hitachi Maru (ship), 156–57
Hitchcock, Babbie, 33
Hitchcock, Jim, 33, 137, 138
Hitler, Adolf, 1, 10–11, 59, 70, 195, 199, 212
Hiyo (carrier), 162, 175
Hodge, Gen. John, 204
Holcomb, Lt. Col. Banks, 119–20, 121
Holcomb, Gen. Thomas, 119

Honolulu, Japanese consulate in, 61–62
Hornet (carrier), 43, 92, 101–2, 118, 123, 124–25, 127, 141
Huggins, Dave, 29–30, 39, 44
Hull, Cordell, 3, 57, 61
Hyakutake, Gen. Harukichi, 122
Hyuga (battleship), 182

ideographs, 17–18, 26, 93
Imperial Navy (Japan), 3, 21, 43, 55, 63, 70, 104
    early successes of, 73
    merchant marine shipping of, 152–63
    security precautions of, 74–75
    See also names of battles
Indochina, 2, 20, 152
Inland Sea, 46, 88
Ironbottom Sound, 127
Ise (battleship), 182
island-hopping campaign, 164–77
    advance to the Philippines in, 175–76
    air and submarine reconnaissance in, 171
    beginning of, 164–65
    naval superiority in, 174
    two-pincer strategy in (1943), 166–67
Isuzu (cruiser), 162
Italian campaign, 206–7
Italy, 206
Iwo Jima, 172, 174, 196–97

Jaluit Island, 170, 175
Japan
    attitude of toward communications security, 75
    educational system of, 18
    envoys of in Washington (1941), 2–3
    "February 26 Incident" and, 136–37
    Neutrality Treaty with U.S.S.R., 6, 208–9
    oil embargo against, 61

Japan (*continued*)
  racial prejudices in, 72–73
  Russo-Japanese War and, 3–4, 35, 88, 136, 139, 189
  See also Imperial Navy; *names of battles*
Japanese-Americans, U.S. attitude toward, 26
Japanese Buddhist Church (New York City), 15, 16, 17, 26
Japanese language, 14–19, 54
  Chinese ideographs, 17–18
  Harvard language school and, 24–45
  phonetic alphabet in, 18
Jimmu Tennō, Emperor, 55, 179
Jintsu (cruiser), 115
Juho Maru (ship), 156–57
Junyo (carrier), 99

Kaga (carrier), 46, 97–99
Kagoshima Bay, 204
Kakuta, Adm. Kakuji, 99
Kalinin, President, 210
kamikaze, meaning of, 179–80
kamikaze airplanes, 192–93, 198
Kane, "Killer," 40
Kanto Plain, 204, 206
Karuizawa (resort), 37
Kasumigaura Flying School, 150–51
katakana (phonetic alphabet), 18, 19
Kearney, James Philip, 14, 47
Kearny, Gen. Philip, 14
Kenkyusha, 96
Kimmel, Adm. H. E., 2, 58, 65
King, Adm. Ernest, 48–49, 92, 122, 132, 142
Kinkaid, Adm. Thomas, 125, 184–85, 188, 190
Kinryu Maru (transport), 115
Kira, Grand Chamberlain, 134, 135
Kirishima (battleship), 127, 129

Knox, Frank, 57, 144, 145, 146
Koch (inventor), 55
Koga, Adm. Mineichi, 149, 162, 166, 170, 173
Koiso, Kuniaki, 202, 203
Kondo, Adm. Nobutake, 100, 123, 124, 125, 128–29, 132–33
Kongo (battleship), 122–23, 162
Korea, 179, 204
Korean War, 121
Kramer, Comdr. Alvin D., 50–51, 52, 57, 59, 64, 65, 66, 112
  OP-20-GZ Memorandum, 58–61
Kroll, Ernie, 29, 43–44
Kuomintang, 60
Kurile Islands, 180, 181
Kurita, Vice-Adm. Takeo, 181–85, 187, 188, 190–91, 192
Kurusu, Ambassador Saburo, 3, 61, 66
Kwajalein Island, 170, 176
Kwantung Army, 20

Lanphier (pilot), 146, 148
Leningrad, German siege of, 70
Lexington (carrier), 85, 86, 165–66
Leyte Gulf, Battle for, 161, 162, 181–93, 199, 203
  beginning of, 181
  crossing the T, 189
  kamikaze attacks in, 192–93
  OP-20-GZ operations and, 182–83, 187, 191
  Ormoc Bay troop landings in, 192
  results of, 191
  U.S. air reconnaissance and, 183
Lingga Roads, 181
Long Lance (torpedo), 154

MacArthur, Gen. Douglas, 8, 84–85, 92, 121, 132, 148–49, 150–51, 175, 201, 204

Mackenzie, 37
McKinnon-san (teacher), 38, 39
McMahon, Comdr. Knight, 169
"Magic," 57, 61, 63, 111, 204, 207. See
  also PURPLE cipher machine
Majuro Island, 176
Makin, U.S. Marines raid on, 165,
  166–67, 169, 176
Malaya, 62, 152
  Japanese occupation of (1942), 40
Maloelap Island, 170, 175
Manchester, Curt, 39
Manchuria, 152
Manhattan Project, 202, 210
Mariana Islands, 165, 171, 172, 174
"Marianas Turkey Shoot," 175
Marshall, Gen. George, 65, 122, 212
Marshall Islands, 164, 165, 166, 170, 176
  U.S. invasion of, 169–71
Mason, Comdr. Redfield ("Rosey"), 49,
  50, 51, 52, 66, 70–71, 73, 77,
  83–84, 88, 97, 98, 104–5, 120, 164,
  212
Matanikau, village of, 110–11
Matsuo, Colonel, 136
Matsuoka, Yosuke, 209
Maude, Gen. Sir Frederick Stanley, 14
Maya (cruiser), 183
Meiji, Emperor, 134
merchant marine shipping (Japan),
  152–63
  convoy system, 154–60
  patterns of, 152–53
  submarine warfare and, 153–56, 160
  tonnage destroyed, 163
  U.S. communications intelligence
    and, 155–56, 162
Michishio (destroyer), 188
Midway, Battle of, 87–103, 106, 112,
  118, 123, 141, 143, 154, 162, 164,
  166, 186, 189, 195, 203

code operation and, 92–103
  results of, 103
Midway Island, 43, 155, 164, 174
Mikawa, Adm. Gunichi, 107–8, 128
Mikuma (cruiser), 101–2, 189
Mili Island, 170, 175, 176
Millstein, Sy, 26, 33, 37–38, 40, 67, 80,
  90, 91, 130–32, 149
Mitchell, Maj. John W., 146, 148–49
Mitscher, Adm. Marc, 145, 172, 173,
  198
Mogami (cruiser), 101–2, 189–90
Molotov, Vyacheslav, 6, 208
Mount Fuji, 46
Mount Niitaka (Taiwan), 46–47
Mount Suribachi, 196
Mount Vernon Academy, 118
Munda Islands, 147
Musashi (flagship), 149, 162, 173, 183,
  199
Mussolini, Benito, 195
Myoko (cruiser), 183

Nachi (cruiser), 189
Naganuma series (U.S. Navy textbooks),
  22
Nagasaki, atomic bombing of, 211–12,
  213
Nagumo, Adm. Chuichi, 88, 91, 96,
  98–99, 100, 164
Naniwa Maru (ship), 156–57
Nationalist China, 120
National Research Council, 67
Navy Department Building, 68
Navy Language School, 119, 213
Nazi-Soviet Pact of 1939, 11
New Britain, 83, 126, 141
New Caledonia, 85, 106
New Guinea, 73, 113, 141, 162, 166,
  171
New Hebrides, 85

Nezumi operations (Battle of Guadalcanal), 116, 121

Nichols, Walter, 29, 66, 112

Nimitz, Adm. Chester, 85, 87, 90, 101–2, 117, 122, 123, 132, 170, 185, 191, 201, 204
  foreknowledge of Yamamoto's plans (Battle of Midway), 91–92

Nishimura, Vice-Admiral, 182, 184–85, 188–89, 191

Nittsu Maru (ship), 157

Nojiri (mountain resort), 37

Nomura, Admiral, 58, 61, 66

Nomura, Ambassador Kichisaburo, 3

North Africa, Allied landing in, 122, 127, 195, 198

Office of Naval Communications, 48

Office of Naval Intelligence (ONI), 20–23, 62, 90

Okada, Admiral, 136

Okinawa campaign, 166, 196–98, 203

Oldendorf, Adm. Jesse, 185, 189

Operation Coronet, 201–2, 204

Operation Olympic, 204

OP-20-G, 49, 57, 61, 93, 213

OP-20-GX, 49

OP-20-GZ Daily Summary, 80

OP-20-GZ operations
  Battle for Leyte Gulf and, 182–83, 187, 191
  Battle of Midway and, 87–103
  distribution of code books, 74
  early operations (spring of 1942), 46–69
  function and responsibility of, 48–49
  Guadalcanal struggle and, 114–125, 133
  IBM "runs," 49, 75–76, 84, 94–96, 99, 119
  island-hopping campaign and, 164–77

  Pearl Harbor and, 54–66
  rank distribution in, 71
  staff members of, 71–73
  wartime expansion of, 119
  See also PURPLE cipher machine

Oshima, Ambassador, 58, 60, 66

Oshima, Baron, 111, 212

Oumansky, Constantine, 59

Ozawa, Vice-Adm. Jisaburo, 173, 174–75
  Battle for Leyte Gulf and, 181, 182, 184, 185, 187–88

P-38 Lightnings, 145

Paine, Robert Treat, 49–50, 52, 73, 75–76, 77–79, 83, 85, 87, 92, 93, 101

Palau Islands, 175

Pearl Harbor, 2, 6, 7, 52, 62
  bombing of, 3, 39–40, 44, 46, 47, 50, 57, 66, 85, 139, 140, 142, 144, 153
  OP-20-GZ and, 54–66
  prior knowledge of, 57–58

Philippines, 8, 20, 40, 73, 86, 166, 173, 175, 180, 185, 203
  U.S. invasion of, 194

Philippine Sea, Battle of the, 162, 173, 186

Port Arthur, 139

Port Moresby, 84, 85–88, 106, 113, 118, 146

Potsdam Conference, 6, 207, 208, 209–11

Potsdam Declaration, 211

Princeton (carrier), 165–66, 183

Puffer (submarine), 159

PURPLE (cryptonym), 54

PURPLE cipher machine, 4, 6, 55–66, 111–12, 180
  "Magic" (intercepted messages), 57, 61, 63, 111, 204, 207

number of, 56
special security measures, 57
See also OP-20-GZ operations
Pyle, Ernie, 198

Rabaul, 83, 107, 170
Ray, Don, 27, 31, 44–45
Reischauer, Edwin, 36–37
Reischauer, Robert, 37
Reminiscences (MacArthur), 148
Rendova Islands, 147
Revolution of 1917, U.S.S.R., 6, 35
Rivera-Schreiber, Ricardo, 57
Roberts Commission, 51
Robinson, Jack, 27, 33
Rommel, Gen. Erwin, 70, 195
ronin (leaderless samurai), 134–35
Roosevelt, Franklin D., 1, 2, 5, 32, 43,
    61, 113, 120, 122, 126, 127, 145,
    148, 181, 207
  death of, 199–200
  declaration of war by, 39–40
Roosevelt, Theodore, 4
Rosenberg, Ethel and Julius, 210
Roth, Andy, 33
Roth, Renée, 33
Russia, 3–4, 6, 35, 93–94. *See also*
    Union of Soviet Socialist Republics
Russian Baltic Fleet (Russo-Japanese
    War), 3
Russian Far Eastern Fleet (Russo-
    Japanese War), 3
Russo-Japanese War, 3–4, 35, 88, 136,
    139, 189
Ryujo (carrier), 99, 114, 115

Sagami Bay, 204
Sage, Comdr. Bob, 169
Saipan, 170, 172
  U.S. conquest of, 202
Saito, Viscount Adm. Makoto, 136

Sakhalin Islands, 181
Samoa, 85, 106
samurai code, 134–35
San Bernardino Strait, 184, 185, 187,
    188, 190, 191
Santa Cruz Islands, 106
Saratoga (carrier), 114, 118
Sato, Ambassador Naotake, 180, 209
Savo Island, Battle of, 107–8, 122
Schaefer, Ed, 28, 43–44, 47–48
Scherbius, Arthur, 55
Scott, Admiral, 122
Second U.S. Marine Division, 170
Sendai Division, 122
seppuku (suicide), 200
Seventeenth Army (Japan), 122
Shaw, Glen, 22–23
Sherman, Rear Adm. Forrest, 192
Shigure (destroyer), 184, 189, 190
Shima, Vice-Adm. Kiyohide, 181, 182,
    184–85, 189, 190, 191
Sho-Go ("Victory Operation") plan, 180
Shoho (carrier), 86
Shokaku (carrier), 46, 85, 86, 87, 114,
    124, 175
Short, Gen. Walter C., 2, 65
Shortland Islands, 126, 147
Siberian Maritime Provinces, 2
Sibuyan Sea, 183
Siegfried Line, 111
Siemer (engineer), 26–27, 38–39
Signal Intelligence Service (SIS), 57, 61
Singapore, Japanese occupation of
    (1942), 40
"Slot," the, 107, 128, 129
Solomon Islands, 73, 85–88, 106, 114,
    116, 133, 137, 141, 162
Sorge, Richard, 59
Soryu (carrier), 46, 98, 99
South Dakota (battleship), 129
Soviet Military Intelligence (GRU), 59

INDEX

Special Attack Corps, 192
Spruance, Adm. Raymond, 92, 96, 100,
    101–2, 170, 174, 186, 198
Stalin, Josef, 6, 11, 27, 59, 181, 207, 209,
    210, 211
Stalingrad, Battle of, 195
Stark, Adm. Harold, 50, 65
Stimson, Henry L., 57
submarine warfare, 153–56, 160
Supreme War Council, 202
Surigao Strait, 182, 185, 188, 189
Suzuki, Adm. Kantarō, 136, 203
Switzerland, 55

Taiho (carrier), 175
Tai Li, 120
Taiwan, 180, 203
Takagi, Adm. Takeo, 164
Takahashi, Korekiyo, 136
Takao (cruiser), 183
Tanaka, Adm. Raizo, 115–17, 126, 128,
    129, 130
Tarawa, U.S. invasion of, 166, 167, 169,
    176
Tawitawi Island, 173
Taylor, Comdr. Rufus, 71
Teiko Maru (ship), 159
Thailand, 62
Theobald, Adm. Robert, 186
Thomsen, Dr. Hans, 59
339th Fighter Squadron, 149
Timor, 171
Tinian, Japanese base at, 174–75
Tinosa (submarine), 154
Tobruk, 70
Togo, Foreign Minister, 208
Togo, Adm. Heihachiro, 3, 88, 136, 139,
    149
Togo, Gen. Hideki, 61, 140, 202
Tokyo, Doolittle's air raid on (1942),
    42–43, 125

Tokyo Bay, 204
"Tokyo Express," 116, 126, 191
Tone (cruiser), 162
Toyoda, Adm. Soemu, 173
    Battle for Leyte Gulf and, 181,
    183–85, 190
Toyokuni Maru (ship), 156–57
Trans-Siberian Railway, 209
Trigger (submarine), 162, 175
Truk Island, 102, 114, 115, 123, 124,
    170, 172, 173, 175
Truman, Harry, 209–10
Tsuruga Maru (ship), 156–57
Tsushima Strait, 3, 88, 136, 189
Turner, Adm. Richmond K., 170
Turner, William, 119
Type No. 97 cipher machine (Japan), 54,
    60, 111
    intricacy of, 55–56

U-boat warfare, 153, 159, 169
unconditional surrender, policy of,
    202–3, 211–12
Union of Soviet Socialist Republics
    (U.S.S.R.), 1, 2, 10, 11, 20, 62, 120,
    180, 195, 206, 208, 210, 213–14
    declaration of war on Japan by, 212
    German attack on, 58–61, 70, 71, 209
    pact with Hitler and (1939), 11
    Treaty of Neutrality with Japan and, 6,
    208–9
U.S. Bureau of Ordnance, 154
U.S. Department of State, 60
U.S. Fifth Fleet, 173–74
U.S. Navy Quartermaster Corps, 40–41
U.S. Pacific Fleet, 2, 47, 62
    at Midway, 87–103
U.S. Seventh Army Air Force, 176
U.S. Seventh Fleet, 184–85, 190. See
    also names of battles
U.S. Strategic Bombing Survey, 213

(224)

INDEX

University of California, navy's language program at, 26, 30, 44

University of Colorado, 44

Ushijima, Lt. Gen. Mitsuru, 197–98, 200

Vandegrift, Gen. Alexander, 116

Van Der Rhoer, Charlotte Whelan, 67, 149–50

Volcano Islands, 196

Wahoo (submarine), 157

Wake Island, 73

Washington (battleship), 129

Wasp (carrier), 114, 118, 141

Watanabe, Gen. Jotarō, 136

Welles, Sumner, 59, 211

West Wall (Germany), 111

Woodruff, Fred, 53, 64, 71, 73, 84

World War I, 2, 34, 139, 145, 212

World War II

  Ardennes offensive of, 195–96

  B-29 bombings of Tokyo in (1944), 196

  end of, 194–213

  island-hopping campaign of (U.S.), 5, 9, 164–77

  Italian campaign of, 206–7

  Okinawa campaign of, 196–98, 200–201, 206–7

U.S. attacks on Japanese merchant marine shipping during, 152–63

  See also names of battles

Wotje Island, 170, 175

Yahagi (cruiser), 198

Yalta Conference, 6, 181, 207, 210

Yamamoto, Fleet Adm. Isoroku, 3, 4, 43, 46, 62, 63, 107, 114, 115, 118, 124, 125, 126, 134–51, 162, 164, 186

  Battle of Midway and, 87–103

  death of, 134, 143–51

  samurai tradition and, 134–36

  threat of assassination to (in Japan), 137

  in the United States, 139

Yamashiro (flagship), 188, 189

Yamato (battleship), 87–88, 141, 173, 198–99, 200, 201

  as kamikaze ship, 199

Yamato (dreadnought), 88

yang and yin, 28

Yenching Institute (Harvard University), 24–45

Yorktown (carrier), 85, 92, 99–100, 123

Yoshihashi, Takehiko, 37

Zuiho (carrier), 99, 124, 182

Zuikaku (carrier), 46, 85, 86, 87, 114, 124, 182, 191